Faith
Can Master
FEAR

Faith
Can Master
FEAR

by

G. ERNEST THOMAS

FLEMING H. REVELL COMPANY

NEW YORK · LONDON · GLASGOW

New York, 10—158 Fifth Avenue
London, E. C. 4—29 Ludgate Hill
Glasgow, C. 2—229 Bothwell Street

To

STANLEY H. NICHOLS

Honored as a physician;
Beloved as a friend,
His devotion to children,
Dispelled many a shadow of fear

Contents

Preface

Any minister, or doctor, or social worker, or teacher—or anyone else who devotes his life to meeting human need—is aware that fear is a constant menace to happiness. It drives men and women to acts which, otherwise, they would refuse to do. It breeds sickness of the mind and body. It often is like an octopus, squeezing the self into helpless submission.

There are many books which have endeavored to describe the causes and available means to find release from fear. This book lays no claim to originality. It is rather the record of the predominant fears which confront the author in his counseling and—of greater importance—the faith which he constantly utilizes as a therapeutic aid. It is a witness of the assurances which give the answer to fear.

Most of the chapters in this book were delivered as addresses before the Learning for Life School of the Haddonfield (New Jersey) Methodist Church. The members of that annual study group deserve a measure of credit for suggesting most of the topics discussed, and for providing some of the suggestions which are incorporated in the manuscript.

I am indebted to my wife for her patient correction of the several chapters, and for the many suggestions which have improved the form. I am grateful also to Miss Esther Pierce for the something more than typing which an effective secretary is able to contribute to the smoothness of a manuscript.

G. E. T.

NASHVILLE, TENN.

I

Fear of the Future

A GROUP OF HIGHLY SPECIALIZED TECHNICIANS, REPRESENTA-
tives of modern industry, had met to discuss their common
interests. Without exception they were college graduates.
Several could boast of a doctor's degree. Most of the group
were young men who had seen foreign service in World
War II. During the evening the conversation turned toward
the future of civilization. Immediately voices were lifted
in rapid succession to make dire predictions. That group of
highly trained men showed that they were victims of such a
consuming fear of the future that it bordered on terror. The
picture which they presented of the probable fate of civilization one hundred years from now was dark in the extreme.

A feeling of anxiety concerning the future is one of
the hardest hurdles which must be overcome by any individual who is seeking to live triumphantly. It wreaks its
greatest devastation on those who try to think creatively
concerning the problems of the world. It presents a danger
to those who are idealistic, to those who try to make a contribution toward a better world society.

What can we do about it? What process of thought can
remove the dark specter which hangs as a shadow over
millions of minds? It is evident that no mere exhortation for
the individual to get rid of fear will suffice. Some fear of the
future is irrational, but much of the current anxiety is a
product of an avid interest in world affairs. It grows out of
knowledge and experience. In confronting this obsession it

11

is evident that we must have a rational and intelligent approach. Fear of the future must be wiped out by a confidence which is born out of reason and faith.

It is wise to remember that desolate fears for the future have been the periodic experience of mankind. In the Book of Isaiah in the Old Testament there is a scene which has been repeated many times in human history. A man who can see no hope for himself, for his country, or for the world cries out: "Watchman, what of the night? Watchman, what of the night?"[1] Sensitive ears can detect clearly the sob of despair which crosses all barriers of time and language.

In almost every age there have been voices raised to reflect widespread fear of the dire destiny of mankind. Often those voices have come from the greatest minds and the most sensitive spirits of their day. Within this century we have already passed through four periods when much of the world was gripped by a fear of the future. In 1914, and the years which followed, fear was rampant because of the separations and sorrows of war. The years 1920 and 1932 were periods when economic uncertainties prompted men to look for a possible end of civilization. Then in 1939–1942 the shadows of war hung heavy again. Fear was common and worldwide.

The entire history of human life on this planet has been marred by these times of terror when people believed that the end had come. Our fears of the future in this generation will not be dispelled by the knowledge that such anxieties have periodically plagued mankind, but that knowledge should encourage us to search for the answer which can bring renewed confidence.

We should be aware that fear of the future often has been brought about by a severe crisis—usually economic or political—which was magnified by close proximity. The Hebrew literature during the five centuries before the Christian era returned again and again to the theme that the end was at hand. Fear of their future had led the people to accept ideas which to them seemed logical because they were so close to destruction and death. The early literature of the Christian Church was filled with prophecies of the end of the world, and of the return of Christ. The crisis through which they were passing, when persecution and death were accepted as the common lot of believers in Christianity, led them to fear the future of the world. Their own hardships made it difficult for them to look far enough ahead to see the triumph of their faith over the very forces which seemed to be bringing disaster.

When the economic crisis came in the United States in 1929 there were millions of people who were troubled by fear. The appalling increase in the suicide rate was only one indication of the agony of mind which shattered the nerves of the people. The future was dark with fear! Many statesmen and practical business men were certain that there was no way out of the economic morass. Hosts of people were afraid. They were so close to the crisis that they could not appreciate the fact that the fundamental assurances upon which the nation had been built were still there. The soil was rich; the natural resources of oil, coal, iron, and other minerals were still abundant. The people were ambitious and eager to work. The land was free of foreign domination. Were not these sufficient to assure a bright future? But the men and women who were so close to crisis and chaos could not see the hopeful factors.

Much of the fear which is widespread at this time is caused by the serious aftermath of war. Our crisis has both an economic and a political foundation. The economic world is uncertain; the political world is tense. It is not our purpose here to discuss these problems. What we do need to understand in facing our fear of the future is that the present situation seems distorted because of our close proximity to it. If we are to judge by the record of history we are forced to conclude that fifty or more years will show that our fear was a foolish waste of mental and spiritual power.

13

It is also true that much of our fear of what lies ahead is caused by a sense of frustration. We want security; we want peace; we want certainty. When we are frustrated in the fulfillment of these desires we tend to identify our failure to obtain them with the fact that the world is awry. We think that civilization is going to pieces because we are deprived of the satisfaction of our deepest longings. Our fears of the future grow. They become dark shadows which hover over life.

Most of the sects which proclaim the imminent end of the world were organized by, and for the most part were made up of, people who felt that life had been cruel. They could not make a go of things economically, or they could not get along with their families and friends, or they did not get the social recognition which they felt their talents deserved. They identified their failures with the nature of the world. It became for them a bad, a cruel world. They were afraid of it.

If we face the matter honestly we will discover that much of our fear has a similar foundation. We feel a sense of failure because the sacrifices which were made during the recent war have failed to bring peace. We had expected that the skies would be clear of economic clouds and political tensions when the guns were silenced. Because we are denied these securities and satisfactions we have a natural tendency to assert that the whole world is evil, and to feel that it never will be better. Hatred for other people creeps into our hearts. We fear them, and the future of all life on this earth.

Here again we need the healing power which comes both from a long view and from a vital faith. The long view will enable us to see that economic changes for the better will be brought about when the adjustments of war are over. Vital faith will enable us to find the peace which comes when we acknowledge that there is a divine providence which shapes human ends.

Beyond these conclusions that our human fears of the

14

future are a periodic experience of mankind, a product of economic or political crisis, or of human frustration, there is something more which must be said. Certain principles are deeply ingrained in the experience of the ages. They can become both an encouragement and a challenge to an individual who is anxious about the future of civilization. They hold the power to dispel fear and to inspire the type of action which is itself a healing medicine for human weakness.

The first basic principle is this: An enlightened minority can save any civilization. Those who live in abject fear of what lies ahead all too often assume that the attitude of the majority must inevitably determine what form the future will take. History makes it clear that nothing could be farther from the actual experience of the ages. Dying civilizations were restored to new life many times by a comparatively small group of people.

The ancient story of Noah and his ark has a truth which is ageless. When the floods come—floods of selfishness, greed, moral degradation, and failure—it is the minority of upright citizens who hold the keys of the future.

It was so in the first century after Christ. Christians were a minority group in the Roman empire. Not only were they few in number, but the great and powerful arm of Rome was determined to destroy them. Yet that minority became the foundation for a new kind of society which outlived the mighty empire of Rome and all its vested power.

It was so in the eleventh century when Francis of Assisi gathered about him a handful of men in whose hearts there was an awareness that their world was evil. Human values had reached a low ebb. But the Franciscans were men of vision. They brought new life to a dying world. They were a small minority, but they had power to change the tides of civilization.

We should not assume that all is dark ahead merely because the majority of people seem to be blind to spiritual values, or because they are deaf to the voice of moral righteousness. The future will not inevitably rest upon the attitudes and actions of the majority. It may be determined by the vision and courage of a small group of men and women who will eventually make their idealism an effective force in changing the pattern of civilization.

However, it is unhealthy for anyone to assume that he stands alone when he is crusading for the right. Maybe he does. But often the individual who fears the future because all the people seem to have forsaken righteousness and godliness has seriously underestimated the number of those who have a like feeling of concern for the welfare of mankind.

When Elijah was held in the grip of fear of the future, the Bible pictures him lying under a juniper tree in the wilderness wishing that he were dead. "All the people have forsaken thy covenant, thrown down thine altars, and slain thy prophets with the sword," he said, "and I, even I only, am left; and they seek my life to take it away."[2] In that hour Elijah heard a voice out of the silence which reminded him that there were many people who had not bowed the knee to Baal. He became aware that there was a host of men all about him who were trying to live by the standards which he was certain had been forgotten.

We look back to the eighteenth century in England as a time of great spiritual revival. Many of those who have an anxiety about our future look back with fond appreciation to that century when, they think, people really cared about each other and about their world. We put a halo about that age as if it marked a high point in human achievement. Yet Bishop Butler gave a different picture when he described the conditions as he saw them in that day:

It is come, I know not how, to be taken for granted by many persons that Christianity is not so much a subject of inquiry, but that it is now at length discovered to be fictitious. And accordingly they treat it as if in the present age this were an agreed point among all people of discernment, and nothing remained but to set it up as a principal subject of mirth and ridicule, as it were, by way of reprisals for its having so long interrupted the pleasures of the world.[3]

16

The eighteenth century does not sound quite so attractive when seen through the eyes of this great leader of religion in that day. On the other hand, the twentieth century obviously stands out favorably by comparison. Religious institutions are flourishing in every part of the world. Almost every village in America has at least one church. More than two-thirds of all the population has some connection with the church. Approximately thirty million people attend services every Sunday.

Not only are the religious institutions supported, but there are other indications of a vital concern for human welfare. Schools, hospitals, assistance for the aged and infirm, and homes for the orphans and handicapped are accepted as a normal part of our society.

There are many reasons, then, why it is unwise for any individual to assume that he is almost alone in his desire to maintain those values which are the hope of permanence for our civilization. He is probably surrounded by a company of people who have a like feeling. But, if those about him seem unconcerned with the common good, let him find courage in the realization that an enlightened minority can save any civilization.

The second principle which should be recognized by those who are in the grip of a fear of the future is this: Men can learn to live together. Much of our uncertainty for the future is centered about the international situation. We fear that nations will again resort to war. We fear the conflict of systems of thought which we assume to be incompatible.

The history of human fear indicates that this point of view has caused greater worry than any other. The earliest records of people who were filled with terror come from the civilizations which were dominated by the obsession that destruction was inevitable because men could not get along with each other.

The development has been slow, often painfully slow, but men have learned across the ages that they could best

17

secure peace and happiness for themselves by co-operating with others.

When man came upon the earth countless ages ago he had to live in fear in order to survive. Every day he met hostility from man and beast. He feared every savage who came out of the forest, perhaps sometimes just to look curiously at his neighbors. It took thousands of years to convince this man that he could trust the families on the other side of the hill, and that he could serve his own best interest by joining with them to make a tribe. It took many more thousands of years before the tribe learned that it could best protect its interest by uniting with other tribes to form a larger unit. It took countless generations before the tribes could learn that their best security lay in the nation. It has taken centuries until the people of the world would even consider the idea of a United Nations.

Every step of the way fear has slowed man down, and prompted him to stay in the old groove as long as possible before adventuring in the new paths of co-operation. Yet the testimony of the ages is irrefutable! Men can learn to live together.

Much of our fear of the future will be dispelled if we accept this fact. The divisions which seem to make a cleavage between the peoples of the world today are minor when compared with the severe handicaps to unity which already have been overcome. It is true that the development of agents of human destruction has been so rapid in this century that we do not have as much time to resolve our difficulties as people have had in former generations. We must quickly learn how to live together. Time is running out for us. The way of co-operation must be found.

The evidence of the ages indicates that a plan for co-operative effort will be found, and will be put into effect. Men can—and, we believe, will—learn to live at peace with each other.

The third principle which will help to dispel our fear

18

of the future is this: The human spirit is supreme. People
for many generations have lived in abject fear of their future because they believed that weapons, or money, or gov-
ernment was supreme. Because they could not control the
power of those weapons, or because they did not possess
enough wealth, or because they had no part in the govern-
ment, they felt helpless and weak. They were afraid.

The Christian attitude toward life is closely bound up
with the idea of the supremacy of the human spirit. "Man
shall not live by bread alone," said Jesus. For him the soul
of man was of greatest significance.

How does that affect the attitude of the individual
Christian who is confronted by a world in which his neighbors tremble constantly with fears of the future? Just this:
He knows that God is the Father of all mankind. He believes
that man is made in the image of God with divine possibilities for life. He accepts the clear witness of our faith that the
human soul is immortal. He does not understand all the
mysteries involved, but he is aware that the noblest witness
of the ages in Christ, and the voices of the greatest of the
philosophers and the poets, are united in proclaiming that
man is made to live forever. He is immortal.

Such a faith in human immortality is a sure antidote for
our fear of the future. Suppose the world is faced with dire
uncertainties; suppose the civilization of this age is headed
for destruction. The Christian soul has within it the seeds of
immortality. The blazing light of such a faith has the power
to dispel even the darkest fear.

Not only does the concept of the immortality of the soul
save the individual from fear of destruction, but it has a
power to transform the seeming impossibilities of a world
into victories for that which is best. Fear of the future often
is based on the idea that material factors are the ruling
agencies in life. But courage often has been a more valuable
factor than an army; love frequently has overcome the

19

strangling power of money; brotherhood sometimes has been more useful than political might.

The human spirit is supreme. More often than we think, it can be victorious over the threats to security and peace which cause us to fear the future. If the human spirit cannot find the means to transform the world in which it lives, it still can seek a better country under the providence of a loving God.

Fear of the future plagues almost everyone who lives in this generation. We wish life might be different, we say, but the world looks dark. Rich or poor, highly educated or ignorant, American or Russian—we fear the future. In those moments when we are given to wishful thinking we long for some miracle to dispel those shadows.

John Bunyan, in his *Pilgrim's Progress*, painted a picture of a world which was held fast in the strangling power of fear. Pilgrim is made to say to his wife: "I am for certain informed that this our city will be burned with fire from Heaven—in which fearful overthrow both myself with thee my wife and our sweet babes shall miserably come to ruin, except (the which yet I see not) some way of escape can be found, whereby we may be delivered."

You remember that Pilgrim began to run with his feet on the Path and his eyes on the shining light which led to the wicketgate. On the journey he was not alone, for the Evangelist met him and guided him.

The fear of the future which dominates the attitude of many men is well described by the experience of Bunyan's Pilgrim. But too few of us accept the light which Bunyan saw. If we walk forward with our feet on the path of righteousness, and with our eyes set on noble goals, we too will discover a strange power and peace to calm our frightened minds. And on the journey we shall find that a divine spirit is leading us. Our fear of the future will have disappeared.

20

II

Fear of the Past

AMNESIA HAS BEEN UTILIZED FREQUENTLY IN RECENT YEARS AS a theme of interest in the plots of books, plays, and motion pictures. The general public has an almost morbid fascination in those twists of the mind which cause people to lose their identity, live sometimes for years a totally different existence, and just as suddenly recover their lost memory. However, amnesia does not occur as often as its use in fiction would indicate. It seldom is the result of a physical blow. When it develops it usually follows a period of severe emotional tension. It represents a means of escape for the mind from unpleasant associations. It is a dangerous attempt to avoid the fear of the past.

Former associations, or mistakes, or tensions frequently leave a permanent residue of fear. The Apostle Paul wrote a letter to his friends in the city of Philippi. When he explained the purpose of his life, he said, "Forgetting those things which are behind . . ." He was aware that blunders of bygone days have a power to wield an adverse influence on the present and the future. He realized that the past tends to place the chill hand of fear on life. He wanted to face the future without this handicap.

When a cross-section of people is requested to list the fears which are making it difficult for them to live victoriously, a large percentage always mentions the strangle-hold of days that are gone. They seem unable to forget the experiences which were unpleasant, or which caused them pain. They are continually hampered by regrets. They are

21

beset by the memory of incidents which make it hard for them to maintain poise and self-confidence.

There are several different factors which contribute to this fear. The first, and most common, is a mistaken understanding of heredity. Two or three decades ago the word "heredity" was unfamiliar to the vast majority of people. Now it is discussed learnedly by the general public whose reading is limited to a daily newspaper. People have been led to assume that their destiny has been shaped in the past, and that they are for the most part helpless before a pattern which has already been set.

Many otherwise normal individuals are obsessed by certain ideas and attitudes which they think they inherited. They feel helpless and afraid. In a course designed to help people with their problems of personality the members of the class were requested to make a list of the fears which gave them the most trouble. Most of the class submitted lists which included a number of specific reasons for their anxiety. One of the cards, however, bore only a few words. A woman had written simply this: "My fear—fear of heredity."

When an opportunity came I talked with the woman about her problem. She was very frank. "I'm not a person who is usually afraid," she said, attempting with great difficulty to maintain her self-control. "Such fears as how to get along with people, or how to avoid inferiority do not trouble me. There is just one thing which keeps me awake nights. Try as I may, I can't get away from it. I'm the youngest of three children. My sister died in infancy. My father and mother and my older brother passed away in their fifties from heart trouble. I'm the only one left. Nobody in my family that I know of has lived to be older than fifty-seven. I'm fifty-two. It looks as if I'm doomed to drop off at any time. Wouldn't that make you afraid?"

She asked the question as if she assumed an affirmative answer. Instead of responding, I asked her a question. "Have

22

you consulted a physician to find out the condition of your heart?"

"Certainly!" she replied. "I have had appointments with several different doctors, some of them specialists. They say that there is nothing wrong with my heart. They tell me that I should be able to live indefinitely. But their words don't deceive me. I have severe pains in my chest, and I know they mean that my heart is giving out."

It was evident that the woman was highly emotional about her weakness. If the other members of her family were like her in temperament, I could easily understand how their emotional drive must have placed a severe strain on their heart action. More than anything else, this woman needed the power of the Christian faith. With that in mind, I endeavored to lead her to the place where she was willing to surrender her future to the care of a loving Heavenly Father. I talked about "the peace which passeth human understanding." To accept and to utilize that assurance was the most important need of her life at that moment. Later, however, we discussed the danger of attributing too much to heredity.

"Perhaps you inherited a tendency toward a weak heart," I said, "but many people with such a weakness are able, by proper care, to outlive supposedly healthy people. Then, also, the human life span is increasing. The mortality age is growing longer with each generation. With good medical care, there is no reason why you should not be able to carry on indefinitely. Your heredity contributes only one part to what you are. It is probably true that the length of your life depends in large measure on you. The doctors think so, and they are almost certainly right."

The best scientific knowledge indicates that it is unwise to assume that any disease is necessarily fatal because of hereditary influences. No one need be victimized by that fear, for it doesn't have a logical basis.

Even more dangerous than the fears of physical illness which are attributed to heredity are those in which it is claimed that such influences control personal habits and modes of conduct. Such a fear is always stimulated when its victim overhears an acquaintance say of him, "He always will be a weakling; he is just like his father."

Nothing could be more misleading than to assume an individual has criminal tendencies merely because one of his parents was at one time involved with the law. There is no basis for the assumption that tendencies toward alcoholism or other moral excesses are inherited. It is impossible to find any trait of character which can be definitely traced to inheritance. Claims for such usually can be found to have their basis in the environment of the child during his years of development.

Dr. Karl A. Menninger summarized the current point of view concerning heredity when he declared that "inheritance is probably confined to physical structures, including brain patterns."[1] Whatever the legacy of the past may include, it is evident that there is no justification for many of the fears that inherited tendencies will cast a shadow on life.

Failures which are actual, or imagined, are the second source of these pressing anxieties concerning the past. We fear the deeds of yesterday because they threaten to become the pattern which we will carry over into the tomorrows. Failure becomes an anchor which holds us back from a life of adventure.

Every one experiences failure. Even the most successful people can vividly recollect endeavors which ended in disaster. Every doctor has indelible memories of patients whom he was unable to help. Every business man recalls certain plans which proved impractical. Every teacher struggles with certain students with whom he is unable to work effectively. Every lawyer presents cases which receive an adverse decision. No one is continually successful. Failure is part of the price which we must pay to accomplish lasting results.

Failure does its most damaging work on the personality

24

when it discourages adventurous undertakings, or when it whispers assurances of defeat. If the reality of the failure can be confronted, accepted, and conquered it can become a source of encouragement. But when the memory of the defeat is kept alive through fear it can weaken and destroy every possibility of progress.

Consider the case of a certain man who has been singularly successful in his business. He deals every day with large numbers of men in labor and industry. He is active in community organizations. He is effective in committees or business conferences where a few people are present. But he is confronted by one serious handicap. He finds it impossible to speak in public. He cannot even conduct a meeting as its chairman.

"I have never tried to speak before an audience since I was thirteen years old," he explains. "As one of the honor students in my graduating class from grammar school I was supposed to deliver a short address. My parents and friends had come to hear me. They were anticipating that I would demonstrate some of my father's ability to speak well. When I stepped to the front of the platform the sea of faces before me became a blur. I whispered the opening sentence in a voice which few could hear. Then I stopped altogether! I couldn't remember another word of the speech which I had worked for weeks to prepare. After an embarrassing silence the people in the audience began to laugh. I went hurriedly back to my seat, ashamed, and hurt. That was the last time I tried to speak in public."

The fear of the past hung over that man's life because of one failure. His effectiveness was limited by his inability to overcome it.

Full and abundant living demands a spirit of adventure. It recognizes that failure is real, but it insists that there is no other choice except to go forward. That attitude was expressed in four lines of verse which had their origin in ancient Rome.

A shipwrecked sailor, buried on this coast,
Bids thee take sail—
Full many a gallant ship, when we were lost,
Weathered the gale.[2]

The fear which has its origin in failure has little power to weaken and distort the life of one who is willing to try to go forward every day to new achievements.

A third common source of such fears originates in unfortunate personal relationships. It is surprising how many people will go to their physician for medicine to cure headaches or high blood pressure, but will steadfastly avoid the fact that the cause of the illness is a family quarrel or a business misunderstanding. Many lives are blighted by the remorse or regret which remains after a man becomes conscious of the fact that he has not acted honorably toward his family or his business associates.

These personal tensions often can be corrected by simple measures. Frequently the dishonorable deeds can be rectified. Often it is wise to confess the mistakes and ask for forgiveness. Too often the regrets one has because of an inability to get along with people remain to create lasting feelings of dissatisfaction.

Sometimes people give evidence of their fear by attempting to avoid those who were involved in the conflict. Then a family tension is often continued for many years without any attempt to relieve the misunderstanding. Frequently the grudge is transferred to other members of the family. All of this tends to create either dissatisfaction with the self, or an air of self-righteousness which encourages a man to believe that others were to blame. Both of these are dangerous to personality. They contribute to an overpowering fear of the past and its associations.

In an endeavor to avoid the shadow of the past many individuals resort to the expedient of making excuses. A young man was evidently infected with a serious case of this kind as he talked of his failure to plan for an occupation or a career. "People used to say that I had the qualities to make a good doctor if I had been willing to study medicine. I would have studied, too, if I had had the money." I reminded him that it was my understanding a relative had promised to pay a substantial part of the cost of his education. He readily admitted that such was the truth. "I guess I would have accepted his offer if I had not been sick the summer after I graduated from high school."

Further questioning revealed that the young man's early experience had left him with strong fears of failure. He had lacked interest in his high-school work. He was satisfied to remain in the lower half of the class when a wise use of his keen mind could have assured him a place near the top. He seemed lazy and self-satisfied. His failure to measure up to his opportunity while in school left him with a lack of assurance. He thought he could not successfully undertake the taxing discipline of a medical education, so he tried to hide his fears in a deluge of excuses.

On other occasions fear of the past is camouflaged by attempts to place the blame for failure on destiny or fate. These escapes from the responsibility of facing reality are readily seized on as the reason for the failure.

The assertion that fate has interfered to decree a certain line of activity is dangerous in the extreme. When fear of past mistakes or shortcomings places a restraint on the possibility of progress we tend to have a false feeling of satisfaction in being able to declare that the failure was predestined or unavoidable.

It is easy and comfortable, too, to cast the blame on some other person. Instead of facing the situation we find it gratifying to be able to explain the defeat by saying it was caused by the handicap which someone else imposed. In international affairs there is a tendency to excuse our inability to make a lasting peace by attributing the blame to some other country. We quickly channel away any responsibility for an undesirable situation when we place the stigma on a convenient scapegoat.

27

In the ancient story of Cain and Abel the murderer was justifiably fearful of the consequences of his deed. It loomed up from the immediate past to cause him remorse. He attempted to explain his feeling of guilt by placing the blame on his brother. "Am I my brother's keeper?" he asked.

The same tendency to avoid blame can be observed in less serious situations. It is a common trait of personality to attempt to escape responsibility when memory creates a consciousness of guilt. Merely to be afraid is to bury the roots of the trouble more deeply in the mind. The possibility of release is postponed. On the other hand, the past has little power to weaken and distort the personality if the victim of the fear is willing to face it.

Putting the matter positively, there is a cure available for those who will make a sincere effort to dispel the shadows of the past. Recollect the agreeable and inspiring incidents in the yesterdays rather than concentrating your attention on its failures and mistakes.

Rodin, the French sculptor, was accustomed to carry about with him a tiny but exquisite piece of sculpture. He would frequently take it from his pocket to study intently its beauty. He declared that he found encouragement for his work by constantly keeping before him this example of the best work which was produced in an earlier age. In a similar manner, each of us is privileged by the miracle of memory to recall the days when life was crowned with success. We can parade such days before us as an inspiration for present needs. To live constantly with thoughts of defeat and failure always allows room for fear to develop. On the other hand, to recollect days when achievements were realized helps us to banish fear and gives encouragement to hope.

The writer of the Book of Hebrews knew that the Christians of his day were terribly afraid. Little wonder when reports came to them from every part of the empire concerning the Romans' persecutions of the followers of Jesus. Many of their friends had been put to death because of their faith.

In this letter the writer lifted before them the moments in the history of his people when courageous faith made the difference between despair and triumph. He reminded them of the victories which had been won by those who faced days of testing similar to their own. He was aware that the fears which had been kindled by persecution could best be driven out by remembering the noble achievements of the early pioneers of the faith.

If our attention is centered on worthy ends, a wise use of memory will help to banish any of the fears which have their origin in failures.

It is at this point that the Christian faith makes a vital contribution to our thinking. It presents an interpretation of the past which is rich in hope for all of us. It traces the long and tedious progress of man on the earth, emphasizing the upward movement of civilization. It points out the trend that is from darkness toward the light, and not from light to darkness. It is a faith which has its foundation in a belief that God is an ever-present help to those who are in need. The past, the present, and the future are all a part of His concern.

John McCormack had a striking and characteristic way of bidding farewell to his friends. At the conclusion of a concert, or when he was leaving on a journey, he would say: "May God keep you in the palm of His hand."

The awareness that a divine agency is at work in the world serves, not only to banish the anxieties concerning the uncertain future, but to dispel as well the shadows of the past.

No one needs to run away from the yesterdays, however unpleasant or difficult they may have been. It is the present and the future which count. To develop attitudes and techniques by which divine and human resources can be utilized for today's and tomorrow's needs is to find the secret by which the fear of the past will be forever banished. A new life of hopeful assurance will then begin.

29

III

Fear of the Unexpected

MANY PEOPLE ARE NEVER ABLE TO RELAX. THEY LIVE CONstantly under the shadow of the unexpected. They do their work every day faithfully and well, but they never entirely escape the fear that an economic depression is close at hand, or that technical advances will make their particular work unnecessary. Even when they go away on a vacation they are uneasy about what may happen. They think the weather will be unfavorable, or that they will become ill, or that the food will not agree with them. If they have children they are always afraid that some accident may happen. The possibility of disaster hangs over them continually.

A metropolitan daily newspaper recently carried on its front page an article in bold type which was filled with dire predictions. It was a summary of everything which might go wrong with America and the world. Printed in italics at the bottom of the list were these words: "All of these may happen today, for it is Friday the 13th."

The newspaper article gave its readers cause to smile, but for many individuals the possibility of tragedy today or tomorrow seems anything but humorous. Every day is Friday the 13th for them. They are beset by the fear of the unexpected.

The writer of the Book of Proverbs said: "There is a lion without. I shall be slain in the streets."[1] There was no real lion in the street. The writer meant that he was confronted by the possibility of evil, of unfortunate and disastrous

30

events. His assumption that he would be slain was a confession of fear. Even if there were danger abroad in his city there was no assurance that it would engulf him. It is evident that this man was afraid of the unexpected.

Such fears have been the common experience of men in every age. We see the "lion" abroad in the threat of sickness, or poverty, or accident, or serious tragedy. We convince ourselves that we "shall be slain," that is, that the tragedy will fall on us.

You and I must learn to handle this fear if we want to live full and abundant lives. The constant specter of possible disaster can destroy all sense of peace, and rob any of us of the satisfactions which we ought to enjoy.

Having admitted that fear of the unexpected is a real problem for many individuals, and having admitted that it takes much of the calm and peace from daily living, let us ask what we can do to free ourselves from its grip. How do we set about to build a life which can be free of fear?

In the first place, remember that the ability to look into the future, and to plan for what lies ahead, is one of the qualities which marks man as superior to the animal. It is the misuse of this privilege in trying to look forward to see everything that may happen, and to plan for every detail in the future which creates the difficulty.

The wise adult will accept as a sacred gift the ability to look back through memory as well as the possibility of looking ahead through anticipation. He will not overemphasize either. He will recognize the limitations of his outlook, and refuse to be under the domination of either the past or the future.

Most of our fears of the unexpected do not materialize. For example, there were many decades during which the common cactus plant was regarded as one of the scourges of mankind. Articles were published periodically forecasting the destruction of rich and fertile lands by this stubborn

31

weed. Reputable botanists saw a tragic future for whole sections of the country as the cactus relentlessly pushed its way forward.

But see what has actually happened! The cactus has become a large source of revenue for thousands of people. It is a valuable source of material for perfumes, soaps, cleaners, rope, and scores of other products. Cactus pulp supplies cough syrups, a heart medicine, and strong alkaloids which may have a big future in medicine. Fifty years ago the cactus seemed to offer nothing to mankind except a barrier to progress. All the fear of the unexpected could have been avoided if we could have seen clearly into the future.

The fear of the unexpected will not haunt us if we recognize that we have limitations in trying to plot and plan for what lies ahead. Whatever we are able to see of the future is only meager. Whole areas are beyond our control. Therefore we are wise if we do not make excessive and dangerous use of this human privilege.

Second, fear of the unexpected is actually a passive attempt to fight life. The greatest happiness is assured to the individual who co-operates with life rather than struggles against it.

Roger Babson declares that he always had a fear of taking ether. He was sure that a tragedy would occur if he gave himself over to the power of the anesthetic. His doctor assured him that many patients have the same fear. "Don't try to breathe in the ether," he said. "Simply blow out the air already in your lungs." Mr. Babson says that taking it that way worked like a charm, for he accepted the inevitable instead of struggling against it.

Fears of the unexpected are an evidence of our attempt to fight life. They are an assumption that tomorrow will be harsh, and cruel, and dangerous. The individual who is willing to surrender himself to the laws of the universe will discover that, while unexpected tragedies do occur, if we maintain a spirit of confidence and assurance, most of our pathway is smoother than it would have been had we wasted our energy fearing the unexpected.

Many parents make themselves miserable by always fearing tragedies for their children. The public school was the bogie for some parents I know. They thought that their children would surely become infected with disease, that the teachers would no doubt give the children false and dangerous ideas about life, that the public school would fail to take the individual characteristics and needs of each child into consideration. They were not exactly certain what evil influence would result for their own children, but they believed that something harmful would happen. They lived in fear of the unexpected. However, after an unfortunate experience in private school they returned their children to the public school system. On that occasion they were counseled to change their outlook. They were encouraged to co-operate rather than complain. They took time to get acquainted with the teachers. As a result, they were amazed to discover the amount of interest which the teachers were taking in the individual child. Those parents began to lose their fear of the unexpected when they endeavored to work with the teachers and the school.

Anyone who desires to avoid and conquer his fear of what may lie ahead will do well to learn to make the best of life rather than to struggle against it. The fighting spirit always fosters a fear that defeat will result from the effort. The co-operative spirit, on the other hand, is not faced with the necessity to secure its own way and can better accept the inevitable rebuffs and defeats which come to everyone.

Closely related to this factor in conquering the fear of the unexpected is the awareness that ahead, just out of sight, more good than ill awaits us. If we recognize this, would it not be reasonable to supplant the fear of the unexpected with an eager anticipation of whatever the future may bring?

In *Cry, the Beloved Country,* a story of South Africa, Alan Paton tells of a native preacher's fear of what may happen when he meets Mr. Jarvis, a wealthy English land-owner. The two families have been involved in tragedy, and Rev. Kumalo has reason to feel that he may receive harsh treatment from Mr. Jarvis. As he mounts the hill to make his call Rev. Kumalo is troubled by fear of the unexpected. He is totally unaware of the friendly welcome and sympathetic understanding which awaits him. Mr. Jarvis says he will send milk to help save the life of a starving native child. He arranges for an agricultural expert to train the native farmers in the rotation and care of crops. He even offers to build a new church for the people of the village.

We often make life difficult beyond what is reasonable by allowing our minds to be filled with fear instead of hope. Life could be rich and meaningful if we were able to see not only the hardships but the happiness which is a part of the unseen future. An aged grandmother told me that she had spent several miserable months filled with fear of what would happen when her granddaughter went from the farm to a large metropolitan city hospital to undertake nurses' training. She had pictured her granddaughter as a victim of every strange disease. She had thought of her as tired and worn from overwork. "What I hadn't counted on," she said with a broad smile, "was her coming home engaged to that fine young doctor."

Many young people have started college with a fear of the unexpected. They have been told that the courses are difficult, that a large portion of the class is dropped every year. They fear the unexpected in personal relationships. Yet most of them find that their college years bring so many hours of enjoyment that these hazards seem insignificant by comparison.

Any individual who desires to overcome fear must discipline his mind to anticipate the rich and fruitful experiences which are in store for him in the days and years ahead.

Then, it is important that we learn to surrender both the present and the future to the loving care of a Heavenly

Father. The unexpected can have no terrors for one who receives each day the support of a God who guides and comforts those who seek Him.

A word of warning is needed here. All our talk of the availability of God's presence and power is meaningless unless the one in need is making a genuine attempt to live honestly and uprightly. We have just reason to fear the unexpected if our conscience tells us that we are not living by the high standard which Christ has set for us. On the other hand, one who is endeavoring to live honestly has the right to look to God for help.

Many successful men in the business world, as well as great leaders of the Christian Church, have learned this truth. For example, John J. Porter, chairman of the Board of the North American Cement Corporation, says, "I have learned not to be afraid of any assignment that conscience tells me I should accept. I have found by experience that, providing I have no motive of personal pride and look at it solely as an opportunity to serve God, He will see me through."[2]

The providence of God can do its effective work of healing in human life if one is willing to have his actions measured by the test of what he knows to be right.

The Bible gives many evidences of the fact that those who know God need have no terror of the dire possibilities hidden in the unknown. All through the ages Christians have been able to face the future with the knowledge that, whatever may come, they have the assurance that God is, and that He loves each one of us. This is a certain foundation on which to build a life.

When Moses led the Children of Israel out of the Egyptian captivity there were many murmurs of anxiety from the people. It was good to be free of the Egyptian tyrant, but what lay ahead? Those who were acquainted with the land through which they must travel were aware that the wind-blown desert offered an almost insurmountable handicap to such a large number of people. Not only that, but already there were reports that the Egyptian army was being organized to pursue them. Who could forecast what agonies would be suffered should the people be dragged back again to their Egyptian prisons? It was then that Moses, filled with the confidence which came from spending an hour in the presence of the Almighty, put new courage into their hearts. He said, "Fear ye not, stand still, and see the salvation of Jehovah, which He will work for you today."[3] The encouragement which Moses gave to the people was well founded. Jehovah did lead them. Their fear of the hardships before them, and of the enemy at the rear, proved groundless. The expected tragedy did not occur.

Many strong and healthy personalities have learned this secret of trusting in the goodness and love of God. It has dispelled the dark shadows of fear, and has enabled them to look out on the future with a feeling of confidence.

Henry J. Taylor, well-known journalist and radio commentator, tells vividly of an incident in his early life when he learned the lesson of trusting in God's goodness. His father was taking him for his first trip down into a coal mine. As the narrow cage began to drop with breath-taking speed into the mine Henry was seized by a feeling of terror. Only the fact that his father had his arms about him kept him from bursting into tears. Down in the mine his father led him by the hand through the dark shafts, sometimes with ceilings so low that they had to creep along. "In this tremendous and never forgotten experience," says Mr. Taylor, "I got very close to my father and also to the Great Father. There in the mine someone asked me if I was afraid and I remember saying, 'Well, I would be awfully scared except my father is with me.' I remember my father looking at me with a grave and yet wondering smile and saying, 'Then you will never be scared, son, because a Greater Father than I will always be with you.' "[4]

Any victim of a fear of the unexpected can find the

miracle of healing if he learns that God is real, and that it is part of His nature to care for those who need Him. When the Psalmist said, "The Lord is my shepherd, I shall not want," he gave a practical and positive answer to fear. The unexpected events of tomorrow need cast no blight on life. The providence of God is broad enough to include each one of us. With His Presence to guide and direct, the unexpected events of the future need cause no anxiety.

When we learn that truth our lives are changed by it.

A young woman was always troubled by fears of what might happen. She refused to believe that her job would continue after the war contracts were finished. She was certain that the future was barren of hope. She had attended Sunday school and church all her life, but she had never learned to make an application of the knowledge she gained to the needs of her own life. Then one day it came to her, as a flash of light, that the promises of the Christian faith were for her. They were not only a part of the historical record as printed in the Bible, but they were for her. She wrote to a friend, "Something very strange has happened to me. I have suddenly realized that I haven't been using my faith. The teaching and preaching have hit me and bounced away. Now I realize that all the worrying that I have been doing is foolish. I'm going to put my life into the hands of God, and let Him lead me."

That young lady has found the secret Christ came to share with each one of us. The fear of the unexpected can no longer maintain a hold on her. She has entered a new and more abundant life.

Fear destroys hope. It maims otherwise healthy minds and bodies. Terror of the unexpected is one of the commonest, but one of the most unnecessary, of these anxieties which have a tendency to weaken personality. A better and richer life awaits those who can break its hold. Once free of the grasp of fear, the future will seem bright with hope, and a more abundant life will begin.

IV

Fear of a Crisis

A SUDDEN CRISIS—AN ACCIDENT OR A TRAGEDY—PUTS A SEVERE test on the individual who is forced to meet it. A friend with whom I was riding stopped his car when it appeared that there was an accident ahead. When we walked forward to investigate we found that two cars had collided, causing nothing more than bumper and fender dents. No one was injured. But the drivers were shouting at each other. They stood toe to toe, brandishing their arms wildly, and threatening what they would do. They both seemed ready to turn violently on the policeman who suggested mildly that they had better move their cars from the center of the highway so that traffic might proceed. They appeared to be successful business men. Under normal conditions they were probably good companions and helpful neighbors to those who were in trouble. But now they were under stress. And fear had changed them.

Fear in an hour of crisis has often led men to do things which they would have considered beneath them in less troubled times. At the hour of the Crucifixion fear drove the Disciple Peter to deny Jesus. Earlier in history, the Children of Israel set up a golden calf as an object of worship when the threat of starvation had brought them to a crisis.

The human body reacts in an unusual manner during such moments of strain. The blood pressure rises, the body trembles, the voice alternates between an angry or pained shout, and a gasping whisper. The individual has a consuming desire to flee from the cause of the fear.

38

It is that urge to flee in times of disaster which has caused some of the severest accidents on record. In Boston several years ago hundreds of lives were lost in a restaurant fire. The grand jury investigation revealed that an excessive use of alcohol was a primary cause. But beyond that the jury concluded, "It is probable that no lives would have been lost if panic had not led the guests to rush madly for the exits. Put down this loss of life to fear."

Not only is there a desire to escape, but medical science reveals that fear in a time of crisis takes its toll in other ways. Dr. James E. Payne tells about a certain man who was "told by his doctor on Monday that he had cancer. On Tuesday he had an automobile accident. On Thursday he had two more. He had never had an accident before. He was so frightened as a result of the diagnosis that he was unfit to drive."[1]

Other physicians have cited cases of individuals who have inflicted injuries on themselves as a result of their fear. Often a permanent heart ailment can be traced to a single time of crisis. Such bodily manifestations as changing the color of hair to gray or white have been observed to happen in a time when fear was aroused by sudden tragedy.

Any individual who wants to be his best will be eager to learn how to prepare for a crisis. Observation of the results of fear in the lives of others should help us to avoid panic when accident or tragedy occurs.

No one is able to free himself completely from the fear which is aroused by sudden danger. Lack of any fear would be a threat to security, and tend to make one insensitive to the hardships of others. But the excessive fear which comes in a time of crisis is unnecessary. It is a sign of weakness. Qualities of personality can be developed which will reduce the wasteful power of such fear.

In the first place, learn to think before acting. The animals act instinctively. They jump, or bite, or run, or snarl, as dictated by their instincts. Uncontrolled fear causes human beings to act in the same way. That's why people run, or tremble, or shout, or fight in times of crisis. Our civilization boasts that it has produced people of intelligence who are able to think through intricate problems. A rational mind is the mark of the gulf which separates us from the highest of the animals. Yet we cannot claim our full right to intelligent human action unless we can make use of our reasoning powers in times of stress. To resort to the animal level of living is a sign of weakness.

Much of the fear which accompanies experiences of sudden peril or sorrow could be controlled if we took time to think. A father came to my office to ask for advice about his son. The young man had spent seven years in college and university preparing for one of the professions. He was revealing a remarkable aptitude for his chosen work. While in the midst of growing success he had married a young woman with whom he had a very brief acquaintance. She proved to be a schemer who had made use of a texture of lies to bring about the marriage. The young man had felt it necessary to resign his position because of her reputation in the town. He turned to another occupation for which he had no training, and in which he was somewhat of a failure. A time of crisis had come when he had no money, no job, and a morally corrupt wife for whom he felt a responsibility. In that moment his fears were driving him to actions which were entirely out of keeping with his customary behavior. As his father described the case, he kept saying, "He's just not thinking." It was evident that the young man's fears had robbed him of the ability to take a reasonable view of his position.

The ability to stop and think through a situation which has been the cause of intense fear often enables us to see that it is not so serious as it first seemed. Many doctors hesitate to reveal the true nature of a disease to a patient because they know that the resultant fears will probably wreak more havoc on the body than the disease itself. If the patient could be relied on to think through the situation, to see that the illness is temporary, or, if it promises to cause a permanent handicap, that some means can be found to build a new approach to life, then the doctor could be completely frank. The doctor and patient together could perhaps work out a solution which would spare the patient a great deal of mental torment. But fear makes a common illness seem the beginning of tragedy.

A right attitude of thought helps to keep life in a proper perspective. When we are tired physically, or when the pressure of responsibility has been large, it is easy then to allow a trivial incident to cause disaster.

> Or in the night, imagining some fear,
> How easy is a bush suppos'd a bear.[2]

The ability to think through a crisis situation helps us to see the important matters as important, and the secondary matters as unworthy of causing upset. Fear in a time of crisis can be controlled, and the individual can be spared much of the weakening influence of shattered nerves and turbulent emotions.

Second, develop a serene mind. Serenity must be cultivated. Few people come by it naturally. Those who are able to maintain a quiet calm in situations which cause others to fear have paid the price of stern discipline.

When a sports writer was forecasting the results of the 1948 Olympic Games he declared that one of the leading athletes on the United States team might have difficulty in London because he lived under high tension before the contest. He was unable to sleep the night before a race. Often during the week before an important meet he could not properly digest a meal. The writer contrasted that athlete with Harrison Dillard, another member of the team. "Dillard must have ice water in his veins," he said, "for he never is troubled by the pressure of competition."

The writer's forecasts proved accurate. The athlete

41

whose performances were accompanied by high tension found the pressure of the huge crowd and the international significance of the races such a load that he was unable to do his best. On the other hand, Mr. Dillard's ability to keep calm contributed to a great victory. He demonstrated a remarkable serenity in times of pressure. Many who applauded his accomplishments missed the fact that his calmness was the result of the sternest kind of discipline. His volatile disposition had threatened disaster many times during his early years. Then he learned the importance of calmness, which enabled him to face a crisis situation without fear.

Practice an attitude of serenity. Suppose you are in a group in which some become excited in discussing newspaper reports of an international incident. Their excitement indicates that they are afraid. If your emotions are under control you do not permit your temper to rise, or lose your quiet assurance. Your calmness is not a cloak to hide a lack of interest in world events; it is rather a demonstration of the fact that you are mature enough not to be stampeded by news which may or may not be true, or which, in all probability, is not significant.

A friend of mine, John Gilmour, has developed this trait to a remarkable degree. He operates a successful dairy farm in New Jersey. While traveling in the West, he was summoned one morning to the phone in the hotel lobby. His father informed him that their huge barns and stables were on fire. "How much are we going to save?" he inquired in a quiet voice. "Nothing!" replied his father. "It's all going up."

"Can you get out the milk to our customers today?" Mr. Gilmour asked.

"Yes," came the reply, "that's all taken care of."

"Sit tight, then, and I'll fly home," the son said.

A few minutes later he was talking with his family. His voice was calm. "They've had a fire at home. Dad tells me that all the barns and stables and dairy houses are gone. I guess we'll have to call off the trip. We're flying home." There were none of the usual evidences of fear. He was able to preserve his emotional and physical strength to help solve some of the problems which had been created by the disaster. His serenity of spirit made it possible for him, not only to be free of the specter of fear, but to use his energies in a creative way.

When confronted by a crisis do not allow your energies to be dissipated by fear, but plan immediately on how you will proceed. Emotional upheaval can rob the body and mind of their strength. But the keenest edge of the fear can be removed if you will look immediately toward the future, and concentrate on its possibilities.

One hot August day, at our summer home in the New Hampshire hills, we felt a breeze spring up, and then the breeze gave way to a wind which swept at gale force through the valley. We took refuge in the house while, for ten minutes, the wind roared with the fury of a hurricane.

When the storm had subsided we went out to inspect the damage. A boy who was passing told us that our neighbor's sheds had blown down. "It's the third time in two years," he said. We walked down to the farm to offer our sympathy, and to lend a hand.

"It surely is too bad about your sheds," we commented.

"Oh, that's all right," our neighbor said, in his usual slow, calm manner. "We'll get busy and build them up. We've done it before; we can do it again!"

That's the spirit which makes for victorious living. When a crisis appears it is easy to let fear paralyze action. If we can immediately plan on a program of rebuilding a barn —or a life—we will discover that fear has lost its power to destroy peace and happiness.

The manner in which the people of Texas City, Texas, recovered from the tragedy of an explosion and fire which took the lives of hundreds of their families and friends, and destroyed millions of dollars' worth of their property, constitutes one of the most thrilling episodes in American history. Thousands of people were victims of fear. But even while the flames were still taking their toll a group of business men conferred with public officials on a plan for rebuilding. The power of fear to complete the task of destruction was turned aside by the discovery that they could go on together as a city.

The individual who is faced by a crisis needs to seek actively to build a new life, or a new home, or a new career. Those who have been willing to make use of such powers as they have at their disposal have always discovered that their problem has been solved, and their fear removed, by a concentrated use of all their abilities.

In one of his prayers before the United States Senate, the Rev. Peter Marshall, chaplain, said: "Let us not be frightened by the problems that confront us, but rather give Thee thanks that Thou hast matched us with this hour. May we resolve, God helping us, to be part of the answer, and not part of the problem."[3]

When we give way to the ravaging power of fear we become part of the problem. We are unable to do our best work, or to realize any of our possibilities. In the hour of crisis an earnest determination to discover a program for rebuilding our shattered lives will not only serve to weaken the power of the fear, but will start the process by which our physical and mental health is renewed.

Finally, when a crisis has stirred irresistible fear, trust in God. Learn the secret that "the Eternal God is thy refuge, and underneath are the everlasting arms." Such a faith is the best antidote for any fear.

Bishop Angie Smith of Oklahoma tells of vacationing in the Colorado Rockies. Before leaving for home he wanted to give the family housekeeper the benefit of a drive through the mountains. For hours they climbed steep highways or dropped speedily into valleys. At last they came to one of those hairpin turns typical of the Rockies. The wheels of the

44

car were close to the edge of the embankment. A precipice dropped off for thousands of feet. The bishop looked back to see if Aunt Miranda was frightened. She was seated in the middle of the rear seat, revealing no evidence of excitement. "Aren't you afraid?" asked the bishop. "No, sir," replied Aunt Miranda, "I'm holding on to the seat and trusting in the Lord."

It is good and practical religion for anyone who is faced with an hour of crisis to hold on to what is left, and to trust in the providence of God.

The last chapter of the Book of the Acts of the Apostles tells a stirring story of crisis on shipboard. Several score of Roman soldiers and their prisoners were sailing from Crete to Italy. A fierce storm arose which threatened the lives of everyone on the ship. Their peril was only slightly decreased when they threw the cargo overboard and cut away the mast and rigging. During the dark hours of the night it appeared that there was no chance for them to escape. The men were frightened. Their cries of terror could be heard even above the roar of the storm. It was then that the Apostle Paul told the captain and crew that he felt certain they would ride out the gale and be saved. "Wherefore, sirs, be of good cheer," he said, "for I believe in God."[4] The calm assurance of Paul did not still the waves, but it stilled the storm raging in the hearts of his shipmates.

Such a faith is able to change any broken, fear-torn life. It depends in part on accepting the promise that God will care for His children. Yet it demands more than an intellectual assent. Many individuals who say they believe in God do not escape the crippling hold of fear. The power of faith to destroy such terrors requires practice. It must be lived. It requires that the individual say, "Now the time of crisis is at hand. I will not be afraid, because I know that God will take care of me. I will surrender my life to His care." The practice of such a faith can break the strangle hold of fear.

45

No one escapes the crisis experiences. They come unexpectedly and bring with them a flood of fears. Unless they are controlled, or unless a plan is adopted whereby their devastating effect can be conquered, they can ruin even strong personalities and steal away every vestige of peace. But you do not need to be a victim of such fears. The practical application of Christ's message can bring the serenity which will assure you of a happy and well-adjusted life.

V

Fear of Being One's Self

MANY PEOPLE WANT TO BE SOMEONE ELSE. THEY WISH IT WERE possible to look into a mirror and see another face. They would like to stand before an audience and speak with the poise and brilliance which others possess. Desires of that kind are often motivated solely by admiration. Athletic heroes have a glamour which appeals to growing boys. Young people tend to identify themselves in their dreams with those they admire. Even people who are older have moments when they wish they could exchange places with someone who has made a marked success of the business of living. At other times they long to be like those who reveal qualities of personality which they covet. People who meet strangers easily, and whose graciousness wins them a host of friends, stir up feelings of envy.

It is a left-over of childhood days that we should want to copy the behavior of those whom we consider attractive. But the experience is real, and must be faced by anyone who desires to develop a triumphant personality.

There is danger in wanting to be some other person if the desire originates in a fear of being what we really are. If we lack confidence in ourselves, or in our possibilities of development, and long to escape into another personality, we create serious conflicts which can rob us of both happiness and peace of mind.

Dissatisfactions with self, the fear that our abilities are meagre and that our material resources are inadequate, the fear that our blundering and failure will hurt those we love

47

—these are at times the concern of almost every individual. It is only when they become so serious that they hinder our progress, or undermine our health, that we need to look for a way of release. If we can find a pattern of thought which creates self-confidence and courage it can contribute an unmeasured satisfaction to any person who is victimized by such fears.

Physical handicaps are the most frequent cause of the fear of being one's self. Alfred P. Haake of Park Ridge, Illinois, describes a physical weakness which threatened his effectiveness. "As a boy I could scarcely talk," he says. "I stuttered so badly that I did not recite in school. I wrote my lessons on paper or on the blackboard. I was underweight, extremely nervous, oversensitive and overactive. When I played ball with the other boys they sometimes called me out when I was actually safe, just to hear me sputter. I knew what I wanted to tell them but it just piled up below my throat and left me mute."

Such a handicap undermined the self-confidence which a happy home and loving parents had tried to develop in him. He was afraid of himself and of his future. Stern discipline and courageous action were necessary before he was able to conquer this fear.

The Apostle Paul was burdened by what he termed "a thorn in the flesh." Biblical scholars have speculated for centuries concerning the nature of the handicap. Whatever it was, it caused Paul to be afraid. He questioned whether he could fulfill his responsibilities to the churches in Asia Minor and Greece while crippled by this infirmity. The spread of Christianity was hastened because he found a God-given strength which enabled him to overcome his weakness.

Set traits of personality which we feel are detrimental are another common source of the fear of being what we are. In telling why she felt inferior to others one woman said, "I never can get over being frightened in the presence of people. I have been that way from the time I was a child. I cross the street to keep from meeting someone I know perfectly well. As for strangers, I will never meet one unless forced by circumstances to do so." This woman is conscious of her weakness. It undermines her confidence in herself, and makes her afraid.

The tendency to indulge in emotional upsets is a further attribute of personality which frequently becomes a source of fear. A few people enjoy losing their tempers. They like the feeling of superiority which comes when people cringe or scatter before their outbursts. Often their loss of temper has produced the same results which tantrums brought when they were children. Those about them gave in to their desires rather than try to silence their outbursts.

A young college graduate told of his experience in an office where he works. "The boss is a driver," he says. "He often goes on a rampage. He comes out of his private office in a rage. He scatters the papers on the desks and shouts his complaints that we are falling down on our jobs. Several secretaries have quit because they couldn't stand his outbursts. But a funny thing happens after he cools down. He evidently feels sorry for what he has done, because he almost always brings in a box of chocolates and leaves it as a peace offering."

This man feels ashamed and guilty. His obvious attempts to compensate for his outbursts by making gifts to the staff are a clear indication that he wishes he were different.

Personality can be made over. Undesirable characteristics of behavior are a challenge to those who are eager for a full life. Discipline and intelligence are required, but unattractive qualities can be changed. Then the load of fear will be lifted.

Another common source of dissatisfaction with self is caused by the fear of making mistakes. Sometimes this anxiety has its origin in the memory of past errors and the unpleasantness which resulted. Sometimes a person does not dare to adventure in new paths for fear he will fail.

When a counselor tries to ferret out the reason for the lack of self-confidence in an individual, he often encounters such comments as, "I'm too careless to do an exact job"; or, "I'm lazy, that's my failing"; or, "I make too many mistakes." The consciousness of such weaknesses often becomes the foundation for dangerous fears. They are injurious to personality because they limit the individual's usefulness, and rob him of possible satisfaction and happiness.

In general, there are two basic reasons for the development of the fear of being one's self. They are a self-centered life, and a lack of self-confidence. While at first glance these two seem to be opposites, both contribute to make fear a genuine factor in life.

The self-centered person must have success in order to be happy. Therefore, any experience which threatens to take away his confidence in himself is dangerous. He becomes suspicious of people. Because his own motives are questionable he doubts the motives of others. He is always afraid of what people will say. He reacts quickly to changing tides of public opinion. His life grows increasingly small as his horizon narrows. His interests revolve about himself. He thinks that is good which contributes to his own feeling of contentment, that is evil which threatens his security or which makes him feel less assured.

Yet these suspicions of people and jealousy of their achievements are evidences of fear. Every boast of one's own attainments is an attempt to bolster a mind which has begun to question whether or not he has failed. Selfishness breeds fear. It fosters a fear of the self which, though often hidden by desperate activity, makes the individual unhappy and dissatisfied.

On the other hand, a lack of self-confidence is often the cause of terrifying fears, especially when the individual becomes obsessed by the thought that he is unable to achieve the goal which he has set for himself. It is because of this factor that physical handicaps frequently wreak havoc on personality. It is disastrous for one with weak eyesight to keep emphasizing the limitations which his handicap places on him. "I cannot travel with ease; I cannot participate in sports; I cannot read or study," he says. Constant reiteration of hardship or handicap makes room for fear.

One who has difficulty meeting and associating with people is not threatened by the ravages of fear until he begins to brood about the matter. If his lack of confidence causes him frequently to compare himself unfavorably with others, or to fondly wish that he could be like someone else, he is feeding his fears.

Our lives can be crippled if we dwell on our weaknesses rather than on our strength. If we are afraid of ourselves, let us search for those ways by which we may find release from this fear, and then we will discover some of the foundations on which a happy life can be built.

First, note that it is useless to talk of being free of the fear of self unless we are prepared to live a life which is tested by high ideals and purposes. Much of the prevalent fear of being what we are is aroused by the awareness that we do not measure up to the best we know. We can never be free from these anxieties while we are weighed down by the consciousness that our deeds are evil or selfish.

It is here that the Christian faith contributes so much to make life worth while. It offers anyone release from the burden of past sin by the miracle of divine forgiveness. In Robert Louis Stevenson's *Dr. Jekyll and Mr. Hyde* we watch Dr. Jekyll's growing fear of that part of his self which has yielded to evil habits. His fear mounted as the chasm widened between what he knew to be right and the actual deeds of his evil self. If Dr. Jekyll could have laid hold on some power to overcome the wicked forces, and have found forgiveness for his past deeds, the story might have had a different ending. His fears would have diminished and the

51

peace of mind which so long eluded him would have been restored.

The Christian faith offers release from feelings of guilt, as well as the power to live uprightly. To accept both of these is to avoid many of the conflicts between right and wrong which inevitably result in fear.

Putting the matter positively, there is strength of personality assured to those who test their lives by high moral and spiritual standards. Their achievements need not be large. Their personal victories may seem meagre when compared with those of some of the people around them. But they possess a poise and contentment which comes from being aware that they are using their strength for worthy ends.

Cyrano de Bergerac is one of the best-loved characters in all literature. Struggling against a great personal affliction, his heroism inspired others to be heroic. Much of his his self-confidence was a result of his choice of the hard right in preference to the easy wrong.

> What would you have me do?
> Seek for the patronage of some great men,
> And like a creeping vine on a tall tree
> Crawl upward, where I cannot stand alone?
> No, thank you.[1]

Cyrano was free from fear because he lived by standards which he knew were noble.

We need not argue about what is right and what is wrong. Argument is too often a cloak to hide an unwillingness to do that which the conscience indicates must be done. Dishonesty, irreverence, and lack of loyalty are mean and low in any generation. If a person wants to be free from fear he must choose what he knows to be honorable and just.

It is useless to talk of being free of the ravages of fear if one continues to be dishonest in his business practices. He can expect no release while he remains morally corrupt. Dissatisfaction with the self gives birth to fear. The fear of being what he is will torture him until the day on which he decides to build a different and worthier kind of life.

Another effective way to drive out the fear of self is to start living courageously. The Bible is a book of courage. It throbs with words of assurance and challenge. "Be not afraid!" "Have no fear!" "In the world ye shall have tribulation, but be of good courage, for I have overcome the world." The Bible is rich in its examples of those who demonstrated by the way they lived that they had overcome their feelings of inadequacy.

The disciples of Jesus came from common occupations. When they first learned what it would cost them to live by the standards which Jesus had taught they went through a period in which they were shaken by fear. In time, however, their fears were overcome. Even the devastating terror of death had no hold on them. Their faith and courage dispelled all their uncertainties.

Every individual who tries to overcome his fears by positive and courageous living soon discovers that many people are quick to advise caution. They warn of the hardships which are involved. The frequency of the discouraging remarks varies with national and international trends. Periods of economic and political crisis inevitably bring more warnings to remain in the conservative path and accept the prevailing situation without protest or struggle.

Even parents are sometimes guilty of attempts—often unintentional—to hold back their children from a courageous action which might rid them of their fears. Dr. Donald C. Laird relates that he polled several hundred high-school students to ask whether their parents generally gave them encouragement in making choices which were difficult. A large majority indicated that their fathers and mothers usually urged caution and discouraged participation in the endeavors or occupations which were unfamiliar.

Courageous and positive action can remove many of the fears of those who are handicapped. Alfred Haake conquered his habit of stuttering by following a daily schedule of corrective exercise. He says, "If you could go back to the old Chicago River you might find an old stump of a tree behind which I used to stand and talk to the woods around me. I still remember the day that I was in the midst of a violent effort when a young man and woman came around the bend and saw me gesturing at them from behind the stump." Mr. Haake's courageous efforts eventually enabled him to overcome the weakness. He is now a dramatic and effective speaker who has been honored by the people of Park Ridge, Illinois, with election as their mayor.

Physical weaknesses cannot always be cured. Sometimes they must be handled less directly. Living courageously may involve discovering new outlets to compensate for those ways of life which are not possible because of physical disability. A young man suffering from tuberculosis of the bone was told that he would never be able to go back to his former occupation. But he learned to work with silver in creating ornaments. While lying prostrate on a hospital bed he makes jewelry and other silver articles, which are in great demand.

It is always essential that the handicap be faced. Fear has little power to cause unhappiness in a life which is directed steadily forward.

Personality traits such as depression, selfishness, or jealousy can also be changed by a determination to live courageously. Individuals who suffer from recurrent spells when they are low in spirits often despair of ever finding the way back to an abundant life. The intense suffering which accompanies their state of mind often results in fears which linger even after the period of depression is over.

Usually, an individual who is dejected must first discover the causes of his weakness before constructive efforts can be employed to conquer it. He may find that periodic depression is a burden which he must accept and live with through the remainder of his life.

Louis Pasteur was a victim of frequent moods of depression. During his early years he was so shy and timid that the neighbors considered him stupid. Pasteur had to fight against discouragement throughout his life. His naturally somber disposition was sorely tried by opposition. Only his firm determination to push forward with his research enabled him to serve mankind so well.

A determination to go forward with a life plan and with efforts to realize one's dreams has solved the problem for many other people. Such common sources of fear as strained relationships within the family group, or dissatisfaction with the progress he is making in business or social relationships, or the feelings which come from the failure to live up to high ideals, can all be handled by one who is willing to live courageously.

The rich young ruler in the New Testament was a victim of fear. In spite of his wealth and social prestige, he was dissatisfied with himself. Then he became acquainted with Jesus, and his own mode of life seemed cheap and tawdry. When he inquired of Jesus what he might do to find peace of mind he was commanded to sell all he had and follow the Master. It was a choice which demanded courage. The young man felt that he could not respond to the challenge. The cost was too great. His affections were too deeply set in other patterns. He returned home still a victim of the fear of being the man he was.

The Psalmist declared, "O that I had the wings of a dove, and could fly away and be at rest."[2] He had a human desire to get apart from the unpleasantness of his world, and from the feelings of dissatisfaction which continually hounded him. He longed to escape. Yet the next day he went back again to take up the struggle. He lived courageously with the power of God to help him.

Most of us have times when we are afraid of ourselves.

55

Every person has moments when it would be a pleasure to possess wings to carry him away from his environment. It is no disgrace to be afraid, and no dishonor to wish to escape from the cause of the fear. But the people who have found true happiness are those who have learned the secret of living bravely with their hardships. They have changed their environment or, if necessary, they have changed their own outlook on life.

Personality adjustment is a tedious and difficult struggle unless divine resources are employed to help in the process. The practice of vital faith makes the task easier because it offers a power which can help. Jesus said to His disciples, "Follow me, and I will make you. . . ." The Christian faith still offers the best and surest means by which personality can be made over. Faith in Christ and the Christian way can transform any person who is willing to surrender his life to the Master's leading. Then every fear of self will disappear. The seeker will learn that there is no satisfaction more enduring than that which comes from a willing response to the challenge to be his best self.

VI

Fear of Insecurity

INSECURITY IS THE MOST PREVALENT OF ALL HUMAN FEARS.
There are few individuals who do not suffer from it at some
time in their lives, and millions of men and women are
never able to overcome the vise-like grip which it continually holds on their thoughts and actions. Many psychol-
ogists list the desire for security as an instinct. Certainly, it
is a fundamental human drive. When security is threatened
any individual tends immediately to be victimized by fear.

In the Sermon on the Mount Jesus discussed certain attitudes toward life which produce unhappiness. "What shall
we eat? What shall we drink? Wherewithal shall we be
clothed?" were questions often asked by the crowd which
followed Him. Jesus saw that their lives were handicapped
by fear. It is a kind of anxiety which has been a frequent
experience of men. It is as old as life on the planet.

Not only is the fear of insecurity common to men of
every generation, but it has always been a cause of tension
and strain. It takes away all sense of calm. It turns otherwise normal individuals into victims of worry. It leads men
to distort values, and to magnify the importance of material comforts, ignoring those things which have eternal
worth.

If ever there was a generation which should experience
a sense of security, it ought to be ours. We have learned to
produce agricultural products and manufacture articles on
a scale never before dreamed of in history. We have cap-
tured the wealth of the mines; we have cultivated the fertile

57

earth to produce food sufficient to satisfy the needs of men. It has become clear that we have the means at our disposal, and the knowledge, so that we can produce enough and to spare.

In spite of our vaunted technical and scientific advance we have not learned how to get along with each other, nor how to distribute the goods which our technical skill makes it possible for us to possess.

> The thing that numbs the heart is this:
>   That men cannot devise
> Some scheme of life to banish fear
>   That lurks in most men's eyes.
>
> Fear of the lack of shelter, food,
>   And fire for winter's cold;
> Fear of their children's lacking these,
>   This in a world so old.[1]

The fear of insecurity often has a tenacious hold even on those who feel that they have a confident faith in the goodness of God. There are few people who are able to escape. Yet from a practical point of view it is essential for all of us to understand the nature of this human trait. No one can live happily who avoids the issue.

Much of the widespread fear of insecurity has its origin during childhood. The haunting longing to be wanted and loved, as well as the requirements of sufficient food and clothing, begin early in life. A heavy blot is cast on the personality when these needs are not satisfied.

It is important for the home and the community to provide a child with the essentials which make for a feeling of security. Little children should never be afraid that tomorrow they will be hungry. They should not have to go to school ill-clothed. Fears of hunger or lack of shelter which become deeply set during those early years are seldom erased.

Relief officials who went to Europe immediately after

the conclusion of World War II found thousands of little children in refugee camps who were dying of starvation. After they had satisfied the children's need for food, they recognized that as the boys and girls grew older, their fears would make them fertile ground for political ideas which seemed to offer a larger amount of security. Someone thought of a simple plan to give healing to their minds. They gave the children pieces of bread as they went to sleep at night—not to eat, but to clutch in their arms like dolls. Hugging this armful of security, they dropped off to sleep with a silent whisper on their lips: "I shall never be hungry again."

Children who grow up in homes where poverty is a constant specter are not the only victims of the fear of insecurity. They are not even in a majority. Poor homes have frequently been the birthplace of greatness. Boys and girls have often gone out of poverty-stricken surroundings determined to devote their lives to help make a better world, or to achieve success in some field of creative endeavor. Hardship has been the driving force which empowered their efforts.

Poverty is only one of many sources of the fear of insecurity which disturb the minds of children. Little ones do not need a large amount of food, nor need it be in any great variety, in order for them to have a sense of well-being. It is when they are unwanted, or when their parents give them the feeling that they are a burden, that children suffer most intensely from the fear of insecurity.

For example, a young man prepared to go away to college. His parents drove him by car to the school on the opening day, and saw him settled in his room before they departed. Two weeks later the boy left the campus without informing anyone of his plans. He hitchhiked his way home. To all questions put to him by his family he replied that he was homesick and could not bear to remain away any longer. The parents finally took him to a psychiatrist for

59

treatment. The doctor discovered that the parents had adopted the boy when he was nine years old. He had come from a large family in which he was an unwanted child. He had never known what it meant to be loved until after his adoption. His new parents had surrounded him with every luxury which affection could provide. They reported that he had never wanted to leave home to stay all night. When he accompanied the family on auto trips he did not enjoy staying away, but always pleaded to return to their own home to sleep. The psychiatrist knew immediately that the young man's flight from college was the direct result of the fear of insecurity which had had its origin in childhood. He was able to make suggestions which aided the young man in making a better adjustment to his situation.

To stave off the crippling force which the fear of insecurity is able to inflict on the life of any individual is a matter which rests in large measure with the parents. They can provide the environment—whether they be rich or poor —which gives a child the satisfaction of knowing that he is loved and needed. Out of such a background he will develop into an adult who feels a measure of security even if economic conditions are difficult.

Because much of the fear of insecurity has its origin in childhood it is not surprising that adults who are victims of such fears can be found in every social class. They are wealthy and they are poor; they are in the business world and in the professions; they live in the country and in the metropolitan centers.

A woman was referred to me for spiritual help. The one who sent her said, "She is a bundle of fears which are ruining her life." As the woman entered my office I was immediately interested in her appearance. She was well and tastefully dressed. She seemed to be a person of culture and refinement. She carried herself with a confidence which must have led many of her acquaintances to conclude that she was a happy, normal individual. The answers which she gave to the preliminary questions made it appear that she ought to have been comfortably adjusted to life. She lived in a large and commodious home. She had two children, both of whom were in college and doing reasonably well. She was working as a saleslady in an exclusive department store. Her husband was in business for himself. She attended church regularly, not the church of her childhood, but another one near by, which was more appealing to her husband.

But when she began to speak of her fears, it was evident that outward appearance and poise were a poor cloak for a mind which was close to the breaking point. Her fears were the fears of insecurity. They had begun during childhood in a home which was constantly rocked by friction. Her misguided parents had reminded her many times that she was unexpected as a baby and unwanted as a child. With the background of her early years the woman would have needed a very favorable environment if she were to live a normal life as an adult. Unfortunately, she had married a man who was able to provide little seccurity. He was one of those individuals who consistently avoid responsibility. He sometimes had work, but often he was unemployed. Money came easily to him, and went just as easily. He was never anxious about tomorrow, always certain that something would turn up which would enable him to get by. This created an atmosphere which was intolerable for a woman who was already in the grip of the overpowering fear of insecurity. Undoubtedly, the husband loved his wife when they were married, and might have surrounded her with the affection she needed, but she felt the overpowering necessity to reform him. She complained and nagged and pleaded with him to secure a steady position, and to provide an income which would satisfy the family needs. Because she could not persuade him to do this, the fears of insecurity which were the heritage of her youth began to increase. She struggled to overcome them, but succeeded only in furthering her dissatisfaction with life.

If this woman was to escape from her fears and to find some measure of happiness, it was evident that she must make several drastic changes in her outlook. For one thing, she would need to build a life with a certain amount of independence which did not rely on her husband. She would need to reduce the number of clothes and other material things which she now felt were essential to her happiness. But more than everything else, she needed the help of God in order to overcome her fears. A plan of spiritual uplift was essential if she were to recover confidence in herself, in her world, and in the undergirding purposes which gave life stability.

During times of crisis, any of us may be a part of that company who are victims of insecurity. But Christ gives us a pattern of how we may live in such a way as to be free of its blight. The resources of practical religion make available both the wisdom and the strength by which any individual can effectively handle fear.

The first principle is to keep life reasonably simple. If our wants are held to a minimum we have less cause to fear economic upheaval or change. Our feeling of security is imperiled when our material desires become more complicated.

A successful doctor began to lose confidence in himself and his future. The basic reason lay in the awareness that his income was inadequate to meet the many demands which were made upon him. A friend counseled him to dispose of his yacht and summer home at the seashore, and to save a larger amount of his earnings each month. He followed the advice and, while he missed the recreation and rest at the shore, he was able to readjust his budget. The added security dispelled his fears and restored his self-confidence.

Our complicated age has placed an immense number of

gadgets at our disposal. They promise to save time and to provide comfort. Men grow more and more dependent on them. There was once a time when the automobile was regarded as a pleasure vehicle. Thousands of owners treated their car as a valuable toy. They took it out of the garage on Saturday morning and polished it in preparation for the family's outing in the afternoon. When the journey was over, the dust was carefully wiped away, and the car was put into the garage for another week. Riding in an automobile now is not a pleasure; it is a habit. The substitution of a privately owned auto for train or electric car as the means for transportation inevitably increases the demands upon a family's budget. The car, the oil burner, the radio and the television, the refrigerator and the freezer, the washer and the ironer— these and many other household articles have moved out of the luxury classification, and have become necessities for the modern family. When these conveniences are unobtainable, hundreds of families are haunted by fears of insecurity.

This is a changing world. In making an adjustment to it there is no positive and sure formula which assures us that we shall have peace of mind. But fear will have less power over our lives if our daily demands are kept at a minimum.

It was this philosophy which motivated Henry Thoreau to conduct his experiments at Walden. He noticed that his neighbors in Cambridge were dissatisfied with life and fearful of the future. He decided that the source of their discontent was explained by the fact that they did not have sufficient money to purchase the goods which they desired, or that they were fearful lest they might not have the means to maintain the standard of living which they had already adopted. He determined to demonstrate to the world that a man could live happily in simple surroundings and with few material goods.

The example of Thoreau is a valuable reminder of the virtue of a life which is not complicated by the possession

63

of too many material things. We have innumerably more gadgets than the people of Thoreau's day. Our fears of security will be less burdensome if we keep life reasonably simple.

In the second place, make such provision for your material security as is practical. Our way of life has always encouraged a citizen to spend less than he earns, and to save a part of what he receives. People who follow that plan have a better chance to keep their minds healthy, because they know they have something laid aside for a "rainy day."

The development of the program of social security has removed a large pare of the stark, foreboding fear which handicapped a host of people. Undoubtedly, there are dangers to individual initiative in a social plan which provides for the unemployment, sickness, and old age of every person. Yet such a program helps to dispel the fear of insecurity. Millions of tortured minds have had their load of fear lifted when they became reasonably certain that in their times of unemployment, sickness, and old age they would have enough for subsistence, and need not be haunted by the horror of what might happen tomorrow.

We must recognize that material security is never absolutely certain. Economic depressions and failures in business have left a sad trail of broken lives. Victims of such tragedies had a mistaken idea that the possession of money alone sufficed to insure security. Financial panics and depressions have seen the tragic end of many fortunes which were carefully built up with the anticipation that they assured security. It is dangerous to rely too heavily on material things for the peace which the mind desires. Yet wise adults will avoid many such fears by making reasonable provision for the future.

Third, keep a proper balance between the spirit of adventure and the dangers which are involved in taking chances. There is a unique satisfaction in attempting something new. Individuals achieve victory, and society advances, as men move out from accepted paths in the search for a fuller and better life. Some personalities are more daring than others. Some people prefer the accepted and familiar way to the less traveled path. But all men have something within them which yearns to progress. Life grows larger as that spirit is expressed in courageous deeds.

Sometimes physical and material security is threatened when a man moves to another part of the country, or changes his occupation, or decides to marry, or to attend college. Life is made up of daily choices. If we fail to accept the challenge to the new and the different we may be able to remain secure, but think what we have missed!

Yet there is a clear line of demarcation between courageous adventure and the urge to speculate. Some proponents of organized gambling argue the virtue of their case by the smug assertion that "all life is a gamble." There is enough truth in the statement to cause confusion. But gambling means taking a chance with factors which are completely beyond the control of the one who makes the wager. The adventurous spirit, on the other hand, assumes that a sufficient expenditure of time and strength may result in victory. The possibility rests in part on how much one is willing to expend of himself. In the case of a reckless bettor the result depends entirely on others, or on factors beyond his control. If he arranges the chances to his own advantage he is no longer a gambler; he is a thief. The betting spirit which depends on chance is always a threat to character and to security. Because it sometimes brings success it breeds false hope. It robs the individual of initiative. An anonymous writer who described himself as a professional declared in a magazine article that the families of consistent gamblers know less where their next meal is coming from than any other group of people. The habit of taking unreasonable chances is the cause of many of our fears of insecurity.

Anyone, then, who would be released from such fears

needs to keep a wise balance between the spirit of adventure and the tendency to take chances.

Fourth, develop a love for people. Insecurity is caused less by a lack of material goods than by not being wanted or loved. The best way to be certain of friendship is to develop an affection and love for people.

A family in a small, mid-west community was severely stricken when both the father and oldest son were killed in an automobile accident while on their way home from work. The widow was left with three small children to support. She had been a good neighbor, and long before the tragedy occurred she had earned the admiration of the community. In the hour of hardship people rallied about her with moral encouragement and material gifts. The woman did not suffer from the customary fears of insecurity. Someone helped her to find a position which enabled her to keep her home and family together. She did not realize it, but her natural gift for friendship and affection had sheltered her from fear during the time of severe crisis.

Sometimes the realization that others have loads to carry helps to keep us from magnifying our own problems. The interest which we devote to assisting those in need allows us less time for introspection and worry. Whatever the explanation may be, love for people is an affective means by which the fear of insecurity can be banished.

Finally, make use of the Christian assurance of God. The Christian faith has enabled men to meet the stern tests which come to people in every generation. Men and women who possess the assurance of Divine providence as an ever-present force in human life have little reason to be tortured by fears of insecurity. The Psalmist long ago developed the theme that God's loving care provides for such anxious moments. He describes one man who successfully faced grievous times by saying of him, "His heart is fixed, trusting in the Lord."

Sickness, unemployment, economic collapse—these and

many other factors enter the experience of men. They leave fears of insecurity which are like a great open wound. The Christian faith is the healing agency which can cure that illness. It provides us with a sense of continuing purpose in life. Even our hardships have a place within the framework of that plan. But more than that, it offers a power by which we can find our way out of the darkest shadows of despair into the light of hope.

Fears of insecurity trouble everyone. But the possibility of applying our faith to resolve those fears is likewise open to all of us. He who is willing to make use of prayer, regular reading of the Bible, and a practical life of trust, can discover a satisfactory answer to all the fears of insecurity.

VII

Fear of People

IN THE TERMS OF MODERN PSYCHOLOY BEING AFRAID OF A crowd is described as ochlophobia. Victims of such fears have feelings of panic when they are among a large group of people. In such a situation they have an irresistible impulse to run away. If they cannot escape they feel weak. Their fear tortures them. It makes a normal adjustment to life impossible. Often they do not realize it, but they are mentally sick. It is an illness which requires skilled treatment. The individual is subjected to grave danger who temporizes with it.

A common and mild form of ochlophobia is experienced by a much larger number of people. Their difficulty is not so much a fear of the crowd itself as it is a hesitation to make choices which will be unpopular with the crowd. The immediate effect of this kind of fear is, of course, not as dangerous as the acute stages of ochlophobia. Often a person's inner conflict is unrecognized by those who work with him, or even by the members of his own family. But the power of the fear to create feelings of unhappiness and of failure is no less real.

The fear of people is often intensified when an individual has a persistent sense of dissatisfaction with himself, or a gnawing feeling of guilt because he has been, or feels he has been, unfaithful to his ideals. The ideals may be those which were taught by his church, or they may be a part of the heritage left by a godly mother or father. When the people with whom he associates, or those whose admiration he desires to encourage, accept a different standard of behavior he is oppressed by the fear of what may happen if he does not conform to their ways. The conflict between the standards of the crowd and the ideals of his heritage is severe. Fear becomes a real and disturbing factor in his life.

Standards of right and wrong have their origin in various sources. Many of our attitudes toward social and individual behavior have been shaped by the teachings of Jesus. Most of us belong in the stream of development which leads individuals to look to the Bible for direction as to what is right. That does not mean that we have lived up to the teachings, for our deeds have often been a denial of the truth which the Bible presents.

Some of our standards originate in social custom. What has been done for many years becomes the norm by which we decide what to do today. In general it is true that long established social habits are an accepted test of right and wrong within the community.

Sir Gerald Campbell, the British diplomat, speaks in his autobiography of the advantages which are enjoyed by the natives of central Africa as a result of their custom of going unclothed, but few of us would be persuaded by his argument to follow a similar course. We would retort that our practice of wearing clothing is necessary, not only for warmth, but for the preservation of values which we regard as essential. Custom has set the pattern which we are satisfied to maintain.

For the Christian a severe conflict occurs when the attitude of the crowd calls for modes of behavior which are at variance with the teachings of the Bible, his church, and his home. The conflict is intensified when the individual becomes convinced that the choices made by the crowd have been dictated by purely commercial and selfish interests.

Many people have yielded to the pressure to follow certain drinking and gambling habits in their homes because of a fear of criticism from the group with which they associate. They are mistaken when they think that such social behavior is necessary to maintain the respect of their neighbors and acquaintances. They fail to take into consideration the truth that all about them are people who are victims of a campaign of advertising which leads them to believe that such social habits are essential to prestige and popularity. Probably many others, also, in their circle of friends, are wondering whether it is necessary to stoop to practices of which they are ashamed in order to maintain their position in the community.

Anyone who wants to be free from the fear of the crowd must learn to distinguish between the actual group opinion and the artificial standards which have been made by subtle advertising. Because healthy and attractive young women are portrayed on billboards as endorsing the use of tobacco does not necessarily indicate that the majority in your community shares that idea. The crowd mind favorable to the use of tobacco has been created for selfish gain.

Because those appearing to be "men of distinction" are portrayed as advocating the use of a certain brand of alcohol does not make it inevitable that the group with whom you associate accepts such an idea as valid. In this case the attitude of the crowd is being created by the prostitution of some men's names for other men's gain.

Perhaps our friends are hoping some member of the group will have the courage to take a stand for what they, too, feel is right. Before we allow this fear of social disapproval to undermine our happiness and lower our ideals we need carefully to examine the situation lest we attribute attitudes and habits to the crowd which misrepresent its honest point of view.

We find the fears which are aroused by the inner compulsion to take a different course from the popular trend in other phases of life, also. Many men encounter it in their business and professional experience. They face a solid wall of opposition to new or advanced ideas. The majority

70

seems indifferent or actively opposed to their concept of what is wise procedure. They tremble before the majority opinion, or they quickly yield to protests against making a change. Many of the forward steps in human progress have been postponed for long years because men of vision were stifled by a fear of ridicule.

Ibsen's *Rosmersholm* tells the story of a doctor who became aware that unsanitary conditions in his community were fostering disease. He laid a plan before the town authorities calling for certain changes which he felt would insure an improved standard of public health. Several prominent individuals in the community were opposed to the changes, including a new sewage system, because some of their tenements would be destroyed and their profits be reduced. These men brought pressure on the doctor. They threatened to ruin his practice if he carried through his reforms. In the end his fears decided his course of action. He withdrew his criticisms, and allowed the village to continue in the filth which caused disease and death.

In every age men have faced situations in which a fear of the crowd led them to shelve their ideals. Nicodemus was one. The Bible says that "there was a man of the Pharisees called Nicodemus, a ruler of the Jews: the same came to Jesus by night."[1] It is evident that his fear of the crowd would not permit him to associate with the Christian group openly. He went by night. Many others have been kept permanently from their noblest aspirations by a fear of what people might think.

Few of the fears which blight life have more power to disturb the mind, or to leave a greater sense of dissatisfaction with the self. When uncontrolled, the fear of public opinion brings a haunting awareness of failure. It develops out of the persistent conflict between spiritual and moral ideals and the choices which are at variance with them. If the fears cannot be overcome they threaten the personality

71

with ruin and defeat. Any possibility of a well-adjusted life is lost.

When you are afraid of people there are several practical ways to approach the problem, ways which have assured personal victory to many other victims of this terror. First, remember that a large part of the ridicule of worthy choices is actually a cloak to hide feelings of inferiority. The people who make up a scornful crowd are quick to cast disparagement on evidences of moral courage if they themselves lack such fortitude.

Jesus of Nazareth demonstrated a remarkable calmness in the face of a hostile mob. Their ridicule did not stir Him to anger. He wept over the city instead of raging against it. His attitude was that of pity for those who plotted His death. We recognize that these signs of courage must be traced in large measure to His faith in the possibilities of men. He looked on their hatred as a manifestation of the fact that they were aware of their own failures. He was free from fear because He realized that many of the people were ashamed, even as they shouted themselves hoarse in anger against Him.

John Wesley amazed the spectators on many occasions by his composure when he was confronted by the hostility of mobs. His *Journal* indicates that his courage was born, not only of a vital personal faith, but of an awareness that the mood of the crowd was created, partly by the attitude of their leaders, but even more by a sense of their own failure.

A young woman described a persistent fear which was making her unhappy. It grew out of the ridicule which she was forced to endure from the people of her social set because of her refusal to follow some of the accepted customs of the group. She described the panic she experienced in being in a gathering of friends, much as she liked them individually. She was encouraged to continue normal social contacts, but to critically observe the group at a time when

72

moral standards were under question. She was to notice indications that some of the people who were quick to scorn the attitudes which they described as prudish were themselves dissatisfied with the life they were leading. The young woman reported that the very fact that she turned her interest away from herself gave her a feeling of confidence. But, more than that, she came to realize that many of the women were dissatisfied with themselves because of the choices they were making.

The crowd which we fear because of its carping criticism is composed of people who have experienced personal defeat. Many of them are attempting to hide their dissatisfaction with themselves by aggressively criticizing others. When one is aware that this is true he is moved to pity rather than fear.

Then, when confronted by fears which result from a stand taken in opposition to the group, try to discover the satisfaction which results from a courageous choice. It is, of course, easy to slip into an attitude of self-righteousness. That frame of mind creates a difficulty of a different sort. But the power of the crowd to hurt and to mar a life is limited when an individual has discovered how worthy choices bring satisfactions of their own.

Cyrus W. Field had to face many heartbreaking defeats during the thirteen years when he struggled to lay the first Atlantic cable. But his failures were nothing as compared with the hostility and criticisms which were hurled at him by those who had invested money in the enterprise, or by the general public which was eagerly looking for a scapegoat to blame. Cyrus Field decided at last to yield to the opposition, and gave up the struggle. He turned his attention for a time to another business. Yet his mind would not give him peace. He braved opposition and further disappointments to establish cable communication between Europe and America in 1866. The opinion of the majority had been rebuked by an adventurous soul whose dreams were stronger than either his opposition or his temporary defeat.

The fear of what a majority of the people may think or do has little effect on one who has experienced the satisfaction of making noble choices. He is relieved from the even greater unhappiness which results from being aware that he has failed to maintain the battle for that which is right.

Furthermore, keep a proper perspective of values. If they stopped to analyze the matter, most young men would prefer the approval of their parents to the cheers of those who frequent the street corner. Most business men would rather have the commendation of their intimate friends than the plaudits of casual acquaintances in the business world. Why, then, should they allow the opinions of such a group to cause fear? Better far is the praise of those whose judgment is most acceptable.

Everyone needs and deserves praise for his achievements. Young men and women should be complimented by their parents when they have made worthy choices. Businessmen have the right to expect that their families will appreciate their efforts to meet courageously the problems of the business world.

If his labor and success are approved, any person will find it less difficult to take a firm stand in opposition to the crowd. Fear will have little power to disturb him. When he weighs the choice of whether to yield to the pressure of the crowd, or to sacrifice the approval of those he admires, he will be induced to make the right choice.

The fear of social disapproval is also less disturbing if we constantly test our attitudes by the example of some of the heroes of our time, or of other days, who battled against heavy opposition to win their victories.

Bayard Taylor wrote:

> When the high heart we magnify,
>   And the sure vision celebrate,
> And worship greatness passing by
>   Ourselves are great.[2]

74

Fear has little power to injure those whose decisions on vocational choices and social codes are inspired by the example of great men. For instance, any one who is an admirer of Lincoln, when he thinks about the courageous battle which the President waged against a hostile cabinet during the tragic days of the Civil War, finds positive and practical help in making his own decisions to hold to what he sees to be right, even when they are at variance with the majority point of view. The young woman who has been stirred by the sacrificial life of Jane Addams or Martha Berry will not find it difficult to voice her opinion against the wrong which is involved in using material goods for purely selfish comforts, disregarding all those who struggle and suffer.

What the crowd on the street corner or in the social set thinks becomes less significant to one whose life is benefited by contact with great idealists, saints, and the heroes of all generations. Courage becomes the only acceptable course of action for such a person.

A Christian has available an even more effective method of overcoming this fear. He accepts life as a trust. He looks to the Creator as the source of his strength. He discovers daily satisfaction in feeling that he is living by God's laws. This consciousness of approval for noble actions, and disapproval for failures to meet moral tests, is an essential part of the Christian religion. The follower of Jesus believes that God is intelligent and understanding. He discovers that the standards of the street are a poor test of right and wrong. To him the laws of God seem more important. He seeks divine approval rather than the acclamation of the crowd.

A vital faith is achieved only by continuous struggle. Unless we keep close to Him through fellowship and prayer we discover that God seems less real than the crowd. On the other hand, a daily walk with the Heavenly Father helps us to have strength to take whatever stand is necessary, even when the opposition is great.

75

John Charles Frémont won lasting fame as a Civil War general, as a candidate for the presidency, and as one of the foremost explorers in the history of the nation. During his career he suffered repeated opposition. He became a victim of constant fears of what might happen if he should follow his own course rather than the will of those who opposed him. Once, in facing this issue, he said to his wife, "If only we could live forever in the heights; . . . the fear and uncertainty would vanish, and we would be as kings."[3]

It is good psychology as well as good religion to live in the heights of faith. By such a vital experience, courage to overcome hardships becomes less an evidence of personal achievement than a result of divine help.

A strong religious faith and trust holds the answer to all the fears which oppress and disturb life. Never is that fact more obvious than when a person is confronted by a fear of the crowd mind and attitude. When you're afraid of people you need to change your outlook. Much of the tension results from facing too constantly in the direction in which the crowd is traveling. Turn your interest and attention to matters of greater importance. Respond to the challenge of your ideals. Then you will find both the reason for living, and the power by which you may live triumphantly.

VIII

Fear of Failure

A CURRENT AND POPULAR BOOK DEALING WITH THE APPLICA-
tion of psychology to the problems of life was the subject of
discussion recently when the radio program called "The
Author Meets the Critics" was on the air. One of the critics
described the book as shallow because it does not recognize
such an experience as failure. "The book speaks of success
and popularity as if there were nothing else in life," he said.
"It would have been a better book if the author had been
willing to admit that many of us have our failures."

Few factors in life cause men more misery than the
ever-present, haunting fear of failure. It stalks those who
have been born to privilege as often as it does those who
face the stern challenge of hardship. It sometimes keeps a
stifling hold on those who appear to be poised and adjusted, as well as on those who are emotionally unstable.

One of the darkest days in the life of Moses came when
he heard the summons to return from the wilderness to
Egypt to take up the gauntlet in behalf of his people. He
recognized that his training in the Egyptian court had given
him a necessary background for the task. He knew that his
body had been toughened by the hard years in Shechem. But
he was afraid! What if he should fail? What if the Pharaoh
should drive him out? What if the people should reject his
leadership? The possibility of failure hung heavily over him.
His fear was so intense that for a time it overshadowed all
the logical reasons as to why he was fitted for such a task.

The fear of failure has a way of casting its blight on

77

many lives. It seizes and paralyzes the best motives and purposes of men. Any individual who earnestly desires to lead a happy and victorious life must understand this human trait, and know how to rise above the fear of it.

Why do we fear to fail? Why are so many men afraid they will not triumph in the competitive system which is so typical of modern life?

It is clear that the contemporary worship of success has often intensified our fears. Dr. Abram Kardiner, a distinguished member of the faculty at Columbia University, has declared that the average American worships success in the way that the men and women of medieval Europe yearned for salvation.

Success is publicized in this generation as never before in history. Magazines and periodicals are alert to search out those who are making an outstanding mark in their chosen professions. They do not attempt to discriminate as to the nature of the achievement. It may be in business, or in the entertainment or sports world, or even in some other less worthy field of activity.

We put a premium on success. To the students in the public schools we hold up high marks as a sign of accomplishment. If one does not reach a certain standard he is looked on as a disgrace. We often make use of a pseudo-psychology to persuade ourselves that failure is unnecessary.

Our glorification of success has merit when it encourages indolent individuals to strive earnestly for some worthy goal. But it tends also to intensify our fear of failure. When worldly success becomes the highest end in life the possibility of not being able to attain it inevitably creates feelings of fear.

The son of a brilliant Christian clergyman had decided to enter the ministry. During his youthful years he was overshadowed by his father's popularity. His father received constant praise from appreciative congregations, and received frequent invitations to serve other churches in larger cities. When the boy began his own ministry he was aware that his family, and even the church he served, assumed that he, also, would be a brilliant preacher. Yet he did not possess the same talents. His ability lay in other channels, but it took him many years to discover that fact. In the meantime he lived in constant fear of failure. He suffered a nervous breakdown, and was forced to take a year off from his work to recuperate.

The young preacher was a victim of our tendency to extol and worship success. This had led him to live for many years with a constant fear that he would fail. Only when he gained a vision of how more humble service was equally important did he regain physical and mental health, and some measure of happiness.

Sometimes our fear of failure is the result of a childhood compulsion which has never been overcome. If a child is subjected to ridicule because of certain mistakes which he makes, or if he is compared unfavorably with older brothers or sisters, he often assumes that he is a failure, or he lives every day in constant fear of it.

Recently I was consulted about a boy of sixteeen whose lack of co-operation was giving his employer a great deal of trouble. He was working during the summer in an amusement center. The people for whom he worked described him as irresponsible, and difficult to handle. Because his father was a public official the manager of the park felt that he could not discharge the boy. He made an honest endeavor to learn why the lad gave them so much trouble. After trying several different approaches he discovered the reason. The boy had grown up in a family which had the cruel tendency to continually find fault. The boy was beaten, shouted at, and ridiculed for his mistakes. In school he had been a problem child from the very first grade. Almost every teacher had assumed that he was a hopeless case.

The manager of the amusement park attempted to give

the lad a measure of affection and understanding. He praised him for any little task which he did well, and endeavored to find ways by which the boy could experience success. In the process his whole character was transformed. He had been so accustomed to think of himself as a failure that he had lost all interest in struggling to do right. His childhood experience had led him to believe that he could not possibly succeed. He had become convinced that his case was hopeless. Because of the constant experience of defeat, he was driven by a fear that he would always fail.

Any individual who feels the destructive hold of failure on his life should carefully reconstruct the experiences of his childhood. The key to the cause of the anxiety may be found in compulsions which have remained across the years to strike fear into what is otherwise a normal life.

The third common cause of this fear is a result of comparisons by which the individual seems to fare poorly. He is left with a feeling of insecurity and the oppressing fear that he cannot make a go of life.

Only a few individuals are troubled by this type of obsession. Most adults have learned through competitive sports and games to take second or third place when necessary. We accept defeat along with victory as part of the lot of those who play the game. We recognize that some individuals have greater skill, and that they can usually be counted upon to win, but we are satisfied to take the position which our ability allows us to have, encouraged perhaps by the knowledge that we have achieved a higher place on this occasion than we achieved previously.

But there are some otherwise successful people who are terrified by the fear of failure. They do not realize it, but they are attempting to win a victory over an older brother, or a school-boy rival, or over a business associate whose attitude on some occasion gave them a feeling of inferiority.

A young woman, a sopohomore in college, was taken to a counselor because she had been troubled by obsessions of failure. These were blighting her life and had made her college years a time of misery. It took only a brief examination to discover that the young lady had an older sister with whom the parents had persisted in making invidious comparisons.

Ruth was pretty. Ruth learned to play the piano. Ruth led her class in school. Ruth made a brilliant record in college. "Why can't you be more like Ruth?" they asked. The young woman had heard it a thousand times.

Her minor victories seemed hollow when compared with the achievements of her brilliant sister. She lived in the atmosphere of defeat, induced by parents who honestly believed that their comments would stir her to greater endeavor. Yet their criticism only served to create a fear of failure from which the young woman could not escape.

When an individual is troubled by such fears it will be helpful for him honestly to face the question whether he is struggling vainly to surpass the achievements of someone else and feels frustrated in the effort. The contented and happy adult is not the one whose accomplishments have exceeded those of his family and friends, but one who is aware that he has made wise use of the powers which he possesses.

In the fourth place, a common fear of failure, which destroys the sense of peace, often originates in a false standard of values. The possession of money and social position are a poor measure of success. Yet many people live in the daily shadow of defeat because they do not have material goods and social position in the degree which they think is necessary for prestige in their community.

There is the case of a man who has a home, fine children, and enough of the world's goods so that he and his family can live in reasonable comfort, and yet is persistently pursued by fears of failure because neither his house nor his bank account are as large as those of his neighbors. This victim of fear is admired by a host of friends. He shares responsibility for leadership in the church and the town. Yet these achievements seem empty shells to him. His neighbors have money and social position of a kind which he thinks he wants. He feels a sense of failure because he does not have them.

Manifestly this man needs to be awakened to a true sense of values. And so, also, do millions of others. No one need have a fear of failure if he is bringing up a fine family, or helping to build a community which places emphasis on strong character and spiritual realities.

It is easy in any environment to allow an utterly false set of standards to mold our attitudes. Young women in college have developed feelings of frustration because they did not have as fine clothes as others. Their wardrobe may have been adequate, but unfortunate comparisons have served to make them feel like misfits.

There must come a time in the life of everyone who is determined to be free of the blight of failure when he will say: "I am no longer interested in a man's possessions or how much power he wields. I am going to break away from the habit of judging a person's success by his popularity, or his wealth, or his property. I myself will try to make some contribution of lasting value. I propose to develop friendships based on common interests. I am going to seek worthy goals. I refuse to live any longer with a constant fear of failure because I cannot always achieve the same ends that others achieve."

Such a confession of purpose will serve as the basis for a more wholesome outlook on life.

There are, also, several positive rules which will help us to face this menace to happiness. First, do not imagine failure if you really have been successful. Many individuals convince themselves that they have made a ruin of life, when actually this is not so.

Often the feeling of failure comes from the tendency to make unfair comparisons. A young man graduated from a small Eastern college and began teaching history in a city high school. As the years passed he was disturbed by a growing sense of failure. On the occasion of the tenth reunion of his college class he returned to meet his old friends. His roommate had graduated from medical school and was already launched in a successful practice. As the doctor talked of his work the high school teacher sank into despondency. The doctor's work was so definite. He was called on to operate on the bodies of people who, a few days later, went out of the hospital cured. The high school teacher compared his lot with that of his former roommate. His income was less than one-tenth of that earned by the doctor. He labored week after week with boys and girls, most of whom were taking history because it was a required subject. They had little interest, and seemed to receive little benefit from it. True, there was a small percentage of the pupils whose faces lighted as new knowledge was given to them, and who wanted to learn more than was required. But these were in a minority. For the most part, his teaching seemed futile. Certainly, his work was indefinite when compared with that of the physician. He came away from the reunion with a growing fear that he was a failure.

Now, manifestly, this man had made an unfair comparison. Certainly the doctor has the satisfaction of being able to help people, and of seeing a speedy and favorable result from at least some of his labors. The teacher did not appreciate the fact that the doctor had his moments of discouragement, too. He did not realize that the doctor often wondered at the value of patching up old bodies when the people went back to the same dissipations and weaknesses and hatreds which had been the cause of illness. On the other hand, the teacher's work, while it was less definite and the results not so immediately observable, might help to shape a civilization. If the work of that teacher makes a few young men and women aware of the lessons of history for our day, and gives them the urge to help build a better world, he will have made a contribution to humanity that may be greater than that made by the doctor.

All of us need to be alert to discover the satisfactions in our own work. The housekeeper in the White House during the administration of President Franklin D. Roosevelt wrote a book about her experiences. It reveals the life of a happy, contented, and busy person. It never occurred to her to compare her contribution and value with that of a United States Senator or a member of the Cabinet. She did not feel frustrated because she could not claim material goods comparable to those of the people who came as guests. She was happy in her work and in her opportunity to serve.

Many fear-driven minds can be released from much misery if they will resist the temptation to imagine failure when they have every right to think of themselves as successful.

Second, the awareness of failure will often be dispelled if we make the best use of what we have. Much of the ever-present concern about defeat is unreasonable. One may actually have made some worthwhile contribution to the lives of those about him. When people are obsessed by such fears it is often because they themselves are aware that they have used only a small part of their ability. They loafed their way through school and college, or they schemed to advance in business. At no time in their lives did they put the best of their interest and strength into their work.

Shakespeare demonstrated his ability to look deeply into the human mind when he wrote:

> Things done well
> And with a care, exempt themselves from fear.[1]

A successful lawyer, who was close to retirement, told me of the fears of failure which had seriously handicapped him during his early years. He had read law in the office of one of the largest firms in his section of the country. He had grown up on the farm, and had neither the knowledge nor

the grace possessed by others who worked in that office.
Soon after he began his studies one of the partners came to
the conclusion that his crudeness would make it difficult
for him ever to be a successful lawyer. On every possible
occasion he reminded the young man of his limitations. He
ridiculed him in private, and scorned him in public. During
the first year of his apprenticeship the young man did inferior work. Other members of the firm joined the carping
critic in suggesting that farming was a more suitable occupation for him. But he refused to admit defeat. "I decided
I was going to be a lawyer," he said. "I determined that I
would do every task that was assigned to me, no matter
how menial, in the best manner I could." In time he convinced even his severest critics that they were mistaken. He
became well-known for the meticulous care with which he
approached each assignment. People learned to trust him,
and to have confidence in his judgment. His concern about
his career was overcome by doing his best with every opportunity which came his way.

There is always a steadying power in completing a task
with all the ability which we can muster for it. Anxiety
about the possibility of failure tends to vanish.

Third, this type of fear has no power to weaken the life
of anyone who accepts his talents as a sacred trust. Jesus of
Nazareth pictured man's responsibility by using a large
farm or estate as an example. Different workers were described as having been allotted certain portions of land.
The owner of the estate knew his men, for he entrusted a
larger amount to some than to others. They were expected
to administer their trusts in such a way as to bring the
owner a reasonable return. They were tested, not by the
total amount which they earned, but by what they did in
comparison with what they had.

Each of us has certain skills and endowments. The
Christian faith proclaims that these are the gift of God. It
reminds us that talents are to be used wisely for the strength-

ening of the individual's life, and for the benefit of the community. If we faithfully apply our abilities to the tasks entrusted to us we may find both contentment and the satisfaction of achievement.

In the final analysis the conquest of the fear of failure is best found in a practical application of Christian principles. God is the creator of all things. His presence is the life and light of men. Each individual is a child of God and, as such, has been entrusted with certain abilities, as well as with the strength to use his skill for the building of the Kingdom. No individual fails who utilizes these God-given qualities to the best advantage, however small his achievements may seem when compared with those of the people about him.

The possibility of failure is a constant threat to happiness. Our competitive society is the fountain of fear which drenches most of those who live within it. The Christian attitude toward life offers a full and satisfying answer to the deepest problems which confront any of us. It leads us to recognize that we have talents, and challenges us to use them wisely and well. It removes the tensions which are caused by an unreasonable striving for position. It opens the floodgates of power from God whereby every one of us can be victorious. In the living of that faith we can successfully avoid the fear of failure.

IX

Fear of Loneliness

"I WATCH, AND AM AS A SPARROW ALONE ON A HOUSETOP," wrote the Psalmist in the Old Testament.[1] What figure could better express the utter helplessness which overwhelms those who are lonely?

The fear of loneliness—of being apart from people for a week or a lifetime—is often a source of unhappiness. It sometimes causes an individual to sink back in helpless despair, or it drives the same person to struggle desperately in the endeavor to escape from his mental prison.

When loneliness envelops a life it must be faced if its victim is to recover a radiant personality. That fact is recognized by anyone who deals with human problems.

The family physician frequently discovers ailments which have their origin in loneliness. Many times in the course of his practice a doctor finds it necessary to say to a patient, "It isn't healthy for you to be alone. Get someone to keep you company. You may then be able to avoid another of these attacks."

A doctor friend told me that for more than two years he made a weekly call on an elderly lady for what she assured him was a necessary check-up. He became convinced that her trouble lay in the fact that she was lonely. She had no near neighbors, and few friends. She was glad to pay the doctor's fee in order to have someone to talk with, someone who was concerned with her welfare. It was her way of escape from the fear of loneliness.

Every minister encounters this fear in his visitations

and counseling. A man close to his eightieth birthday came to talk with his pastor about the major problem of his life. He had an unmarried daughter who was in her fifties. She had kept house for him ever since her mother passed away twenty-eight years before. "My daughter has a fear of being alone," he said. "She has never wanted me to be away over-night, so I have never taken a vacation except when she was with me. She doesn't have many friends. She seems to be happy enough taking care of me. But all the time I notice how frightened she is when she is alone. I'm getting along in years and may drop off at any time. I wanted to ask for your advice. What plans can I make for this daughter of mine? How can I spare her the agony she will suffer when she is left alone?"

Ministers are constantly called on to assist in cases where this kind of fear has been a determining factor in making for unhappiness.

Often the most intense cases of loneliness occur in the great metropolitan centers. The fact that an individual is surrounded by a host of people does not solve the problem. As a matter of fact, more people, proportionately, tend to be lonely in the city than in rural communities. But loneliness can be a disturbing element wherever one happens to live.

There are many reasons why people are lonely. Not the most common, yet one of the most difficult to handle, is that which a man or a woman experiences because of the choices which he has made. The Apostle Paul felt that kind of lone-liness. He wrote to his young friend Timothy, "No man stood with me, but all men forsook me."[2] He had pro-claimed a principle which he felt was necessary to human happiness and right in the sight of God, but men had not supported him. No one in the group had the same ideals, and so he felt alone.

The most difficult fear of this kind to understand and to cure results from an unfortunate relationship between par-ents and children. A baby is entirely dependent on its mother. As it grows in body and mind it learns to decide between certain courses of action. That is part of the process of growth. Some parents feel that their affection for their child entitles them to guide its every activity. They think that their love is demonstrated by the manner in which they shelter the growing boy or girl from the normal give-and-take of life, or from the necessity to make choices. Sometimes these distorted signs of affection are an outlet for unconscious desires in the parents which have no normal expression. When such solicitous interest is prolonged beyond childhood or youthful years it produces feelings of dependency which are often disastrous. Even in his adult years the product of such an environment can never escape the unconscious need to be with his mother. Because he is separated from normal social relationships he is continually haunted by a fear of loneliness.

Consider the case of a young man who is successful in business and popular with his associates. He appears to have every quality which should contribute to make him happy. Yet he is troubled by fears of being alone. When he talks about his problem he says that several times each week he attends parties or visits with friends far into the night in order to avoid going to the rooming-house where he lives. In his room he is haunted by loneliness. He has no interest in building friendships which might result in marriage and a home. He wants to realize such a goal, but he is unable to bring himself to have more than casual interest in other people.

Inquiry concerning his background revealed that this young man is the oldest of two children. During his early years his mother felt a growing disappointment because her husband became so absorbed in business and club activities that he had little time for his family. She had turned to her baby boy to find an outlet for her longing to be needed. She had sheltered him; she had pampered his every desire; she had kept him from many of the normal activities of a

89

growing youth. She had maintained such a grasp on his emotional life that he could not escape. Even after her death he was unable to get away from her influence. It was a remarkable tribute to his courage that he had made fine progress in business and in many normal social contacts. But he was always lonely without knowing the reason for it. This fear marred his life until he was given an opportunity to understand its cause, and to follow a plan of procedure which promised release.

Many of the prevailing fears of loneliness have a similar origin in an unwise dependency of a child on his parents. Anyone who has a real desire to achieve emotional freedom must rid his mind of such dark shadows. It is wise to lift up the cause of fear to the light of understanding. Any of us can handle loneliness better if we understand its origin and cause. Then we are in a position to follow a plan which will help and heal.

The steps by which the mind can be freed are easily listed. They are not difficult to understand. However, the nature of the fear often makes the adjustment seem formidable. Harsh discipline of the mind and body is essential. The hopeful factor in the situation is that the results of such discipline are almost certain to be favorable. A vast company of well-adjusted individuals can witness to the fact that the fear of loneliness can be banished from any life.

The first step is to cultivate normal social relationships. Broaden your circle of acquaintances, and deepen your friendships. That is not the entire answer to the problem, but knowing and caring for people will go a long way toward lifting the burden.

Many individuals who are troubled by loneliness find it difficult to handle their personal relationships. Friendships are rare. They have a natural diffidence in the presence of strangers. They are timid in making new acquaintances, and hesitant about giving the encouragement which would deepen the acquaintance into friendship.

Almost everyone shuns the necessity to meet people. That is perhaps the most important single fact to be recognized by those who have difficulty in their social life. The one whom you look upon with envy because of the easy way he has of greeting strangers has probably cultivated that quality over a long period of time. Genuine struggle may be hidden even now by his confident manner. It is a basic characteristic of people that they are hesitant in meeting strangers.

Margaret Lee Runbeck admirably illustrates this human trait in an incident which she relates concerning her graduation exercises from high school. As the valedictorian of her class she had been assigned a seat on the platform next to the guest speaker. When the class advisor suggested that she carry on a conversation with the honored guest it seemed more than could be expected of her. "I'm supposed to talk wittily to you," she whispered with what she describes as a delirious smile, "but . . . but . . . I haven't a thing to say. I'm scared to death."

"I'm scared, too," the speaker answered quietly. "I've got a speech written down, but I don't think it's much good, and besides—"

"But YOU don't have to be afraid," said little Margaret.

"Neither do you," the speaker replied. "I'll tell you a secret; then you'll never need to be scared again. Everyone on earth is shy, self-conscious, and unsure of himself. Everybody's timid about meeting strangers. So if you'll just spend the first minute you're in the presence of a stranger trying to help HIM feel comfortable, you'll never suffer from self-consciousness again. Try it."

Margaret Runbeck declares that she has made use of this plan on many occasions. She testifies that it works unfailingly. The speaker who gave the advice was famed for his skill in making new friends. At the time he addressed Miss Runbeck's graduating class he was Assistant Secretary of the Navy. Later he was elected President of the United States for four consecutive terms.[3]

The question of how to develop a technique for meeting people is only a part of the problem. That is necessary and important. But the best weapon to use against the fear of loneliness is the proof that you have the qualities which make a good friend. Sympathy, honesty, and fairness soon help one to earn the love and esteem of all with whom he comes in contact. There are some individuals who think that providing expensive entertainment, or traveling with the "right crowd," is the way to make friends. Such means are a shallow substitute and almost always end in disappointment.

In the Old Testament both David and Jonathan grew up in surroundings which made them victims of a fear of loneliness. Jonathan was the king's son who, because of his position in the court, was not permitted to make normal friendships. David had been taken from his home in the country and plunged into a world which was foreign to him. Both were lonely. But they discovered an unrealized happiness in the friendship which grew up between them.

A sense of utter hopelessness concerning life often envelops people who are alone. It tends to disappear if the proper human relationships are cultivated.

Closely related to this essential need for fellowship with others is the healing power which comes from a life of service. The fear of loneliness gets its strongest hold on those who have never learned to take an interest in movements for human betterment. The selfish, self-centered life is always ready prey for fear.

The Christian Church offers countless opportunities for service. Let a woman take a Sunday School class of little girls and learn of their enthusiasms and hopes. She will discover her circle of interests broadening. Life will take on a new fascination. Let a man teach a class of high school boys and share in their interests. His responsibility as a teacher may take him to the high school football games, to violin and piano recitals, to concerts by the glee club, to track meets, and to circuses. His horizon will be broadened, and his life will become less lonely. There are many such opportunities in the church. Men's work and women's societies, clubs and classes for youth of all ages, these and many other interests provide a rich opportunity for service.

Every individual can help in his community, in some capacity. There are a multitude of opportunities in public welfare—in the Community Chest, the Boy and Girl Scouts, the Red Cross, and the Y.M.C.A. or the Y.W.C.A. The important matter here is not the place where the service is rendered, but that the individual should actually do it. Loneliness has far less chance to hurt a life which is being used for the assistance of others.

There is still another factor which helps to remove the blight which the fear of loneliness casts on life. It is to learn the delight to be found in moments when we are alone. The present-day world gives us little opportunity for solitude. People work together. Apartments throw families into closer proximity than was true in an earlier generation. The radio invades the privacy of every home with its high moments of entertainment as well as with that which is crude and revolting. Modern society makes it difficult for anyone to be alone.

It is healthy at times to be apart from the world. Jesus often sought the quiet and solitude of the mountainside after a busy day spent in ministering to the sick and needy. The clamoring crowd was far away. He did not find it disturbing or frightening to be by Himself. Indeed, He came from those moments of seclusion with renewed strength to face His responsibilities.

The late Irvin S. Cobb told of an occasion in his life when he discovered the delights of being alone. He had lived through hectic months in a newspaper office. His telephone had rung constantly. His door was always open to those who were quick to absorb his time by taking advantage of his friendliness. Usually, at such times, he would go away with his family, or with a group of friends, to enjoy recreation and rest. On this occasion it was impossible for his family to accompany him. As an alternative, he decided on an ocean voyage and several weeks visiting in the English countryside. He kept away from the places where he might have come into contact with newspaper associates. When the experience was over he declared that those weeks of solitude gave him a new outlook on life. He recovered an appreciation of values which had long been forgotten.

Of course, there is no virtue in being alone if you cannot endure your own company. Many of the pressing fears of loneliness have their origin in a dissatisfaction with self. Whether it is justified or not, the individual is often harassed by a consciousness of failure. Under such conditions the last thing he wants is to be alone.

Many well-adjusted adults have made the discovery that loneliness has less power over them if they can get away for a time from the pressure of the world and enjoy the privilege of rediscovering lost values.

The final secret to a life free from the fear of being alone is found in an application of religion to the problem. Such fears are dispelled when one cultivates the presence of God. Jesus said, "Lo, I am with you always, even to the end of the world."[4] Again, he said, "I will not leave you comfortless; I come to you."[5] The Christian religion gives assurance that any individual may experience a close and intimate fellowship with God.

It is manifestly impossible to have this experience when faith is weak. Nor can one know these high moments if his conception of God makes no allowance for a divine spirit with whom he can know a personal and real fellowship.

Usually one is best prepared for high spiritual adventures if he accepts the fact that the nature of God is revealed in Jesus of Nazareth. God then becomes personal. He

can and does take the form of the Christ as presented by
the writers of the New Testament. It is easy to think of a
close fellowship with a God who is like Him.

When loneliness has left us frustrated, dissatisfied, and
anxious, it is our privilege to seek a daily walk with the
Heavenly Father.

> When fears depress,
> These mortal fears I cannot quite repress,
> For all my faith and trust—O Love divine,
> Hold Thou my hands. [6]

Such a comradeship answers many of the longings for assurance and understanding which seem lost to one who has
been a victim of fear.

Loneliness is a periodic menace to happiness. However
well adjusted to life, or however rich in loved ones and
friends, the stark shadow returns again and again to remind us that life is incomplete. Sometimes the shadow never
lifts. Loneliness remains a haunting agony from which we
never escape.

This fear need not cast a cloud on an individual or his
home. Cultivate the possibilities of friendship, human and
divine. As you do that, the load of loneliness will be lifted.
You will then have banished one more of the shadows which
first threaten and then maim an otherwise happy life.

X

Fear of Life

"FAIN WOULD I CLIMB, YET FEAR I TO FALL!" SIR WALTER Raleigh scrawled those words on the window pane of his cell while he was a prisoner in the Tower of London. There were steps which he might have taken to assure his freedom, but he was afraid to make the attempt because of possible reprisals by his enemies at court. He languished in prison, hoping every day that some friend would take the lead in securing his release.

Other men who are imprisoned by their environment hesitate to climb to their desired freedom because of the fear that they may fall. They are aware that the fear robs them of their right to an abundant life, but they find it more comfortable to accept defeat or failure than to struggle for the realization of their hopes.

The fear of facing life is the thief that steals more worthy dreams and high ideals than any criminal who ever walked the earth. It frequently destroys the chance of a happy marriage. A bachelor uncle came to speak to a radiant young couple at their wedding reception. "So you are going to live in one room and both work?" I overheard him say. "Yes," replied the bride, "we'll get along somehow." "Of course, you will," continued the uncle quickly and positively. Then he became wistful. The young couple were too absorbed in their own happiness to notice the change in his voice. "I once had the chance for a day like this," he went on, "but I was afraid to go ahead on my small wage and what seemed a poor opportunity for advancement. It was the biggest mistake I ever made."

Such a fear of facing life deprives some men and women of the opportunity of marriage, but it deprives many others of advance in business or in their profession. Occupations which offer the satisfaction of life-long desires, as well as the privilege of service, have been lost because of the fear of facing life.

A young man went to his minister to say that he had decided to make the Christian ministry his life work. He showed enthusiasm for the task, and declared that he felt "called" of God. When he discovered that preparation for ordination required seven years of university study his enthusiasm began to wane. He was afraid that he could not measure up to the challenge. He was counseled as to the means by which his education could be financed, but such encouragement was not sufficient. He preferred the mediocrity of a position which required no training to the demands of a long period of study. He was afraid to face life.

Educators who have the responsibility of training young men and women for science, or medicine, or law, often discover those who are unwilling to pay the price to secure the necessary preparation for these professions. They fear that they cannot pass the examinations, or that the adjustment will be unpleasant. In almost every office or factory there are those who can advance to places of larger responsibility if they face the fact that the opportunity is waiting for them, and that they must work to realize the goal. But they are handicapped by fear. They are afraid that the extra efforts will be wasted because they will go unnoticed, or that others will be critical of them, or that they may not be able to carry the responsibility if promotion does come. It all adds up to a fear of facing life.

The danger to the mind which results from a constant refusal to accept life's opportunities has long been recognized by clergymen who labor in the pastoral relationship. Physicians also have pointed out the results which are observable in the human body when individuals constantly refuse to face life. They have stated that physical illness sometimes causes mental unrest, and that mental unrest frequently produces physical symptoms.

Stomach ulcers are often an evidence of emotional upset. They usually result from a steady diet of ideas or thoughts which eventuate in tension or fear. The analysis of the international situation by newspaper columnists or radio commentators in such a way as to create hysteria is one common cause. So, also, are anxieties about the economic situation, or the personal problems which come from family or vocational tensions.

A physician stepped into a hospital corridor with me after we had stood together at the bedside of a business executive. "That man would not be here if his secretary had destroyed the morning paper every day before he had a chance to see it. He is one of the thousands of casualties in this post-war world." This man of affairs is brilliant, intelligent, and admired by a host of friends, but his fear of facing the world, and the critical international situation, had poured poison into his body.

Continued emotional pressure is another common cause of the fears which result in stomach diseases and many functional ills from which men suffer. During the tense days of the 1948 baseball season a player with a Boston team was sent to the hospital suffering from ulcers of the stomach. He was reported to be twelve pounds under weight and a victim of intense emotional strain. Day after day the load increased as the season progressed. Every play became important; every time at bat was a severe test. He was aware that a single mistake might mean the loss, not only of a game, but of a season's work. His illness was an evidence of the price which any individual may be called upon to pay who lives under such pressure.

98

The fear of facing life may cause not only disappointment and failure but, accompanying them, such physical symptoms as ulcers, colitis, high blood pressure, and, even in some cases, heart ailments. The price is too great. This conclusion is inevitable when we realize that fear is a parasite which can be conquered.

Studies have recently been completed which indicate that many industrial, household, and traffic accidents are caused by the unconscious desire to escape from a situation regarded as dangerous or unpleasant. Fear of facing life forces the mind to seek for methods to avoid that which is a hazard to the self or to society. Dr. Flanders Dunbar of Columbia University Medical Center has published two comprehensive books on the subject. "Since at least four million of the fifty-five million workers in the United States are killed or disabled every year, susceptibility to accidents ranks high on the list of unsolved problems confronting medicine," she declares. She goes on to state that a study of accident patients reveals the fact that the vast majority have health records which are far above the average. It is when they are subject to undue strain, or when they are motivated by the fear that they cannot measure up to the demands placed on them, that accidents happen.

To be involved in an automobile accident, or to be struck by a street car, or to maim the hands in a machine, is a poor kind of escape from life, even if it is done unconsciously. How much better it is to learn to understand the fear which is driving us, and to cultivate the means by which that fear may be channeled toward constructive ends.

In meeting the stern challenge which comes from a fear of facing life it is first necessary to admit that we are afraid. No good is accomplished by hiding from the truth.

Jeremiah stands out as one of the noblest figures in the Old Testament. The rôle of prophet was not easy for him. When he felt the call to go before the people he compared his strength and ability to those of a child. Jeremiah many

99

times indicated in his writings that he was troubled by fears. But the very fact that he admitted that he was afraid gave him a foundation on which he could build a life of faith. After he had acknowledged his weakness he was able to dip into available spiritual reserves, and to go out confidently to meet the challenge of adversity.

Many people will not admit even to themselves that they are afraid to adventure in new paths, seek out new friends, or make a radical change in their mental outlook. They scorn the idea that they are afraid of anything. But their refusal to make an attempt to change their approach to unpleasant problems is abundant proof that they are controlled by fear. The first step on the road toward mental and spiritual recovery will come when they admit their weakness.

A young soldier wrote from the Pacific during World War II:

I have naturally had experiences in which I have been afraid. Public speeches in high school and college, conferences with employers before and after obtaining a job, the first serious talk with that certain young woman—all these have caused me to be scared, and greatly so. But in the majority of experiences I have found that a person must admit either outwardly or at least to himself that he is scared, then compose himself and win his battle. I do know that the advice to "admit it!" is as appropriate and right when you are facing an assault in battle as when you are trying to sell an important person some insurance. It has been proven time and time again out here that the men who failed to admit their fears are the ones who crack in battle. But if you admit that you are scared, and don't try to fight it, then you are on the right road to overcoming your fear.

In his observation of men at the time when they were tested by the hardships of war this young soldier confirms what we know to be true of those who are living in a more peaceful environment. Anyone who is controlled by a fear that is limiting and distorting his life needs to admit it. Get

100

it out into the open. The worst of its influence will be dissipated if we are willing to face it.

The most satisfying power to heal minds which are afraid to face uncertainties is found in right thoughts about the meaning of life. It is derived from the ability to see life whole. Such an understanding is best found in the Christian point of view. For those engaged in ordinary, everyday activities, who are finding the pressure more than they can bear, no other system of thought offers a comparable hope.

Christianity is an affirmation concerning God. But it is more than that. It is a way of triumphant living. For the Christian, God is not alone the Creator who supplies the energy by which the sun, the moon, and the stars are kept in their courses; He supplies also the energy which is the source of all life on the earth.

Go a step further to note the implications of this faith. The Christian faith declares that God is like a father in His relationships with men. The human-divine relationship is best understood by comparing it to a family. God is the father; we are the children. As children, each one has a heritage which includes material goods, as well as personal characteristics and possibilities. We are expected to administer those gifts as a trust. Life tends to become full and abundant when we use them wisely.

These concepts, when applied to any human relationship, help to drive out all fear. For example, see how they dispel the fear of changing an occupation. The Christian who regards his abilities as a trusteeship which he must use wisely and well weighs the new opportunity from the standpoint of that trust. He is not handicapped by any of the fears or anxieties which trouble others if he can honestly conclude that he has talents enabling him to meet the challenge of a more responsible position. He has no room for fear when he sees the new adventure as a fulfillment of his duty to God.

The application of the Christian faith works in other

101

situations as well. Consider the case of the school teacher who had always wanted to travel, but who could never master the courage to make a start. She had found it pleasanter and more comfortable to remain at home each summer. She was afraid of new surroundings and of the necessity to make new friends. Her outlook was entirely changed when she came to regard the earth and its treasures as gifts of God which she was privileged to share. The majestic beauty of the Grand Canyon, or the ancient wonders of Egypt, or the friendly intimacy of the English countryside are all treasures which, by her peculiar position, she is able to see. She is no longer afraid to adventure into new surroundings, because she accepts her privilege as a sacred trust. Whom she must meet, or in what strange cities she must live, are now of small concern. She accepts all of life as a trust, and is thankful for the opportunities which are available for her use.

Life is not a destiny which is rigid and unshakeable. It is a series of glorious possibilities out of which we are privileged to shape our future. Not all individuals have been endowed with talents by which they can win high honors or public acclaim. Many people achieve their desires while rendering faithful service in lowly positions. The important consideration is the willingness to accept and carry out such obligations as are given to us. The fear of facing life has little power to disturb those who are consumed with a desire to serve others.

The Christian faith does more than challenge us to make full use of our abilities. It offers spiritual power for effective living. It invites us to seek from God the guidance and strength which we need to meet the summons of adventure in new and difficult surroundings.

In the early days of Hebrew history we are told that Abraham heard the call to move out of the land which had been his heritage and home. He felt the urge to make a break with the familiar surroundings of his youth. In that moment he was handicapped by fear. It was difficult to turn his back on the past, even when he knew that the decision was right. It was more comfortable to remain where he was. His was the age-old fear of facing life. In that hour he found a strength which banished his uncertainties. It came from an awareness of a divine power which directed and guided him. The Bible says, "The word of God came unto Abraham in a vision, saying: Fear not, Abraham, I am thy shield and thy exceeding great reward.[1]

Such spiritual resources are available to every victim of this fear. They offer the power by which personal victory can be assured.

A successful architect relates that as a boy he became the victim of a fear which was to mar his life. When he failed to face up to it the tendency to run away developed into a habit. For a time it seemed certain to defeat any possibility of normal living. He graduated from college only by practicing the sternest discipline. Every day demanded a hard fight. After completing his studies he went into business in Philadelphia with a firm of architects.

The fear continued unabated. It made concentration on his work difficult. One day the senior member of the firm called the young man into his office to inquire about the weakness which had become apparent to every member of the staff. The young man explained that he was troubled by such severe headaches that it was almost impossible for him to work. He declared that he knew that he must have been called into the office to receive his discharge, but that he had already given thought to resigning.

The senior member of the firm made no reply for a time. When he spoke it was to request his secretary to bring from the files a set of plans. He spread them out on his desk.

"These are the plans for a large public building," he said. "They are the finest plans ever drawn in this office." Then he opened a desk drawer and took out a copy of the New Testament. "We draw plans for buildings," he continued, "but this little book does something more important. It draws the plan of a good and happy life. You have read it before, I know, but read it again. You may find the blueprint by which you can make your life over."

The young architect found the answer to his needs. It came partly from the Bible, and partly from his contact with the radiant personality of his senior associate. Life began over again. It was a life which was free from fear.

Many other victims of fear have been helped as they have accepted the daily strength which is made available through faith. It is faith in the providence of God, and in the availability of His power to meet every need.

Fear to face life hampers a countless host of men. They have ideals and dreams, but their fears make the realization of the dreams impossible. They allow opportunities, and friendships, and faith to slip away because they are afraid. The answer to such fears is within the reach of all those who desire it. Face up to your fears; discover the possibilities which God has entrusted to you; and then make use of His power to live victoriously.

XI

Fear of Being Young

WHO IS AFRAID OF STAYING YOUNG?

That seems a reasonable question. We generally assume that everyone wants to remain youthful. "Why should people be afraid?" we ask. On the contrary, many men and women seem willing to go to any extreme in the endeavor to preserve the appearance of youthfulness. Some follow a strict diet to keep them slender. Men will search out a tailor who claims that his suits restore a youthful appearance. Women will haunt fashion shops for clothes which encourage the illusion that they rightfully belong to the younger set. Men and women alike cling desperately to activities which foster the idea that they are still young. Why, then, do we think there are any who are afraid to keep their youth?

The answer is evident to those who study human nature. People are caught in the grip of this fear because the demands on young men and women are so numerous. For one thing, youth is active. Youthful years are a time of going, and doing, and being. They are a time of playing and working, and adventuring. Many adults find it much easier to sit and to listen than to share activity. They find it more comfortable to watch what is going on than to take a part in it.

This generation enjoys observing sports and games. There has been an extraordinary increase in recent years in the recreations which appeal to the spectator. Crowds cheer at the football games, often there are long lines of people

105

waiting to get into the motion picture theaters, and every evening millions tune in on radio programs. The development of television offers another mode of escape from the demand that we actively participate in recreation.

Roman society was aging rapidly when the people were satisfied to be observers of the vast spectacles in the Colosseum. They found it more comfortable to watch the games than to share in the sports. The custom of active participation became one of the forgotten memories of Rome's vigorous youth.

Perhaps we believe we want to hold or recapture our youth, but if we are content to watch life rather than take an active part in it, that unwillingness to participate is a sign that we are controlled by fear.

Then, many people have a fear of being young because youth exacts a price by making it necessary for them to confront and conquer their prejudices. Youth has no prejudice—unless it is that older people have set ideas from which they refuse to budge, in spite of facts which indicate that change is essential.

Christianity has always been a youth movement. It was first a summons to young fishermen by the Sea of Galilee. It has continued to make its appeal to young men and women in every generation. Christ proclaimed a religion which left no room for prejudice in the lives of His followers. Any type of Christianity which stirs hatred and parades its self-righteousness is far removed from the religion of Jesus. Jesus declared, "Ye have heard it said in olden times, but I say unto you. . . ." He used the same phrase a number of times in the Sermon on the Mount.

The religion of His day was old. It was steeped in prejudice. He summoned men to a new and more noble outlook on life. No wonder his message appealed to youth! It called men to lift from their minds the stifling load of prejudice.

Youth has always been characterized by this broad outlook. It accepts no fixed assumption about life and the course it must follow. It asks questions, marshals facts, and proposes solutions. The adult mind often has already become set in its way of thinking. It takes for granted the fact that the pattern of life worked out in the yesterdays will be satisfactory for the tomorrows. To be forced to once more investigate the matter would be painful. To change decisions already made would be intolerable. So we find that many men and women are afraid of keeping young because they would be forced to confront and conquer their prejudices.

There is nothing peculiar in the fact that progressive movements in politics have usually commanded the enthusiastic support of youth. Youth notes corruption, dishonesty, and the inability of governments to function for the common welfare. It has no mental set toward traditional parties, or party organization, and is not opposed to an idea merely because it is untried. When we are unwilling to confront new ideas we reveal a fear of staying young.

The fear is even more disturbing when it is aroused by the necessity to meet and understand those who have been raised in an environment and culture quite different from our own. Young people have no prejudice against a particular race or nationality unless it has been induced by their parents or older people with whom they associate.

A kindergarten child always talked about Amenia when she described the happy times she enjoyed at school. Before a month had gone by it was evident that Amenia was her favorite playmate. When she spoke of the little friend her eyes were shining. Then something the child said stirred suspicion in the parents' minds that Amenia might be of a different race from that of their daughter. "What color is Amenia?" asked her mother. "I don't know," she answered, "I haven't noticed,"

The youthful mind accepts the Negro, the Oriental, the Protestant, the Catholic, or the Jew. It judges him as an individual, without regard to his color, race, or religion.

A business man talked frankly about the necessity he found to revise certain preconceived ideas. His daughter is a student in one of the large Eastern women's colleges. She has become convinced that it is imperative that minority groups within the community have equal opportunity. She brings her father evidence of the contribution which Jews have made to the progress of the world. She talks of the Negro as an equal rather than as an inferior. Her father said, "I have been forced to reconsider my prejudices, and I don't like it." With his advancing years, he has discovered that his outlook has grown narrower. Now he has been called back to the youthful point of view. He is afraid that keeping up with the ideals of the young people will be difficult for him. It is hard to break away from prejudices which have become deeply ingrained. However, life will be richer for him because he has made the effort.

Closely related to this is another reason why many adults fear to stay young. They hesitate to put forth the effort to keep on learning. Youthful years are the time of adventure in books and ideas. Young people are eager for knowledge, and profit from the experience of learning. No characteristic of youth is more evident.

After completing his preparations for the final examination in a history course, a young man closed his book. "I have read my last book of history!" he exclaimed. "I'm glad to be rid of it!" He didn't realize that this is the point of view which leads one toward an early old age. The observation that he has learned all that he plans to learn, that he is not eager for further knowledge, indicates that he is losing the spirit of youth.

Many of us resist the idea that we should keep learning. We assume that we know all that is worth knowing, or at least all that it is necessary for us to know. We miss the thrilling adventure of contact with great books, or the recent discoveries in science, or the miracle of a new plant or flower.

Farmers in several Eastern counties were invited to a day's session at which time agricultural experts from the state bureau were giving instruction concerning the latest methods being used on dairy and poultry farms. One farmer explained his refusal to attend the sessions by saying: "I reckon I won't go. I'm thinking they may have some new ideas, and I'm too old to bother now to change my way of doing things."

Many adults reveal an attitude which is similar to that of the farmer. They are afraid of knowledge. They fear the obligations which knowledge will place upon them. They might be forced to change their mode of life. Wherever an adult refuses to keep learning you find an individual who is afraid to stay young.

Granted, then, that the fear of accepting the youthful point of view is common to large numbers of people, what can we do about it? Is there a plan of life which will enable us to develop those qualities which have kept others young? What are the drives which will make us desire to participate in life rather than to observe it? What will enable us to confront and conquer our prejudices? How can we stimulate the desire to continue learning?

Manifestly, there is no simple formula, like a medicine which can be taken in simple doses after every meal. It is a question of an attitude of mind. It may be that a complete renovation of preconceived ideas is essential. Whatever may be necessary, the following steps are basic in any effort to drive out this fear.

First, guard against every tendency to be satisfied with ease at the expense of action. The human body quickly adjusts itself to inaction if it is not urged on by the will. The easiest choice which anyone can make is to do nothing, or to do as little as possible. That is particularly true when the vocational occupation has been settled and hours of leisure have been determined. Then the individual tends to follow a pattern which places the fewest possible demands on his body.

The rapid increase of heart ailments in this generation has led doctors to conclude that this feverish age is placing too much demand on the human body. Many individuals are hurrying too fast and for long hours each day. Such conclusions are irrefutable. Some adults need to learn how to slow down rather than how to hurry the pace. But it is the larger group of people who are growing old before their time by allowing their bodies and their minds to vegetate who are obsessed by the fear of staying young. They can enter a new and richer life by turning away from habits of inaction.

John Wesley declared that vigorous and active service for others is one of the secrets of eternal youth. In his *Journal* he wrote:

June 28—I can hardly think I am entered this day into the seventy-eighth year of my age. By the blessing of God, I am just the same as when I entered the twenty-eighth. This hath God wrought, chiefly by my constant exercise, my rising early, and preaching morning and evening.[1]

That kind of life requires stern discipline. It means choosing the hard road instead of the comfortable chair. It involves willingness to respond to each challenge which comes. This is not easy, but it brings a full and abundant life, and drives out all fear of being young.

In the second place, avoid the common tendency to criticize other people. The Psalmist said, "Blessed is the man that sitteth not in the seat of the scornful."[2] It is an easy seat to occupy. It is comfortable and satisfying. To sit in that chair removes part of the stigma from our own failures. When we can find fault with others our own mistakes do not seem so significant.

A high school boy was talking in the locker room to a

group of his friends. "I just overheard some of the girls," he said. "Boy, were they taking people apart! Nobody in the school will be left with any character when they get through. They sounded like a flock of old hens." The boy meant that word "old." Carping criticism is associated with being old. The youthful spirit does not stoop to malign and injure.

The prophet Elisha towers high among the great figures in the Old Testament. He made so noble a contribution to the religious life of his day that his faults seem minor. But Elisha had a tendency to complain. He was quick to note the failures of those who, had he been willing to trust them, could have been counted on for staunch support. He turned in anger upon the group of children who were making fun of him. Elisha's critical nature marked him as an old man.

Just and constructive criticism is always acceptable. We profit by receiving it. Others may profit as we give it. But the tendency to magnify the weaknesses of our associates easily becomes a habit. If we allow it to develop into a trait of personality, we cannot maintain the spirit of youth.

Furthermore, people seldom have a fear of being young if they live with a hopeful outlook. William James said, "Be not afraid of life. Believe that life *is* worth living, and your belief will help to create the fact."[3]

There are many people today who firmly believe that the world is evil, that international relations are moving inevitably toward war. The discovery of atomic power has added to the mournfulness of their predictions. They are convinced that all others are inferior to the citizens of their own country, and should, therefore, be subject to their will. Unfortunately, people with this philosophy are now found in almost every nation.

Men and women with the youthful vision recognize that there is still hope of straightening the tangle of international relations. While they recognize the difficulties and

111

disappointments involved in the attempt to promote understanding among the nations, they look hopefully to the day
when good will will find the answer. They assume that there
is a like desire for peace in the hearts of people in every
land. They are eager to find opportunities for friendliness
and co-operation.

It was Thomas Hardy who challenged his readers to
maintain the hopeful attitude toward the world and its
problems. He wrote:

> Whence comes solace? Not from seeing
> What is doing, suffering, being;
> Not from noting Life's conditions,
> Not from heeding Time's monitions;
> > But in cleaving to the Dream
> > And in gazing at the Gleam
> > Whereby gray things Golden seem.[4]

It is not only "solace" which comes from gazing "at the
Gleam." The youthful spirit is kept alive, and fear is dispelled.

When the Children of Israel were preparing to enter
the Promised Land twelve spies were sent out to examine
the new country and to bring back a report concerning the
soil and its produce. They returned with samples of the
luscious friuts which they had gathered. But ten of the
men reported that it was unwise to go into the new country
because of the size and numbers of the inhabitants. They
saw the people as giants and themselves as grasshoppers.
The minority report was given by Caleb and Joshua. They
urged immediate advance. While recognizing that hardships would certainly follow, they looked at life with the
light of hope in their eyes. The Bible tells us that Caleb and
Joshua were young men. Theirs was the youthful spirit
which enabled them to look beyond the shadows of fear to
the light of a new day.

Live with hope for the tomorrows if you want to remain young. Fear will vanish, and you will discover the

joy and satisfaction which has always come to those who worked earnestly to make a better world.

Finally, keep alive spiritually. You can do it if you are willing to follow a simple and direct plan. The first step is to read the Bible every day. As the textbook of the Christian faith, the Bible gives the key to truth as well as the secret of abundant living. It brings the reader into contact with God, and with many of those men who, in the past, have been able to maintain a close relationship with the Eternal.

Then, practice the habit of prayer. Recognize that the Divine Presence is available to strengthen each individual who comes into contact with Him. Prayer is the means of approach. It is the line through which the power flows from the source to the place of individual need.

Anyone who is spiritually awake will never have a fear of the youthful attitude and outlook. He will not seek to escape from life and its responsibilities. He will be an active participant in the struggle for a world in which there are justice and equality of opportunity. He will maintain the far look which sees beyond the immediate hardships to the possibilities of a better tomorrow.

Living eagerly and working vigorously, there will be no room in his thoughts for fear. His will be a rich and satisfying life.

XII

Fear of Growing Old

MANY OF THE COMMON FEARS WHICH DISTORT AND MAIM LIFE are unrecognized by the family and friends of their victim. He goes his way, outwardly calm and assured. He does his work without revealing the terrifying thoughts which keep him awake during the night, or which steal into his consciousness many times every day.

The fear of growing old, however, is often evident to others before it becomes known to those who suffer from it. Many people grow old naturally and gracefully. They are often impatient with people who do not make a similar adjustment to life. Yet they themselves may reveal in their unconscious strivings the natural resistance to bodily changes which comes with the years.

Sometimes the signs of growing old are the cause of the most intense fears which an individual can experience. He may have accepted economic crisis or personal disaster bravely, but he feels helpless before the relentless advance of time and the consciousness that the physical powers of which he was so proud are beginning to fail.

A woman famous for her beauty in the court of King Louis XIV of France retired to a convent at the age of thirty-two because she feared the approach of old age. She had no particular concern for spiritual matters, but she wanted to escape from the court before her face lost its youthful beauty.

Many other individuals, although they have not let it completely overpower them, have felt in their hearts the same emotion. They have feared that the arrival of a certain age meant that life for them was finished.

Should the process of growing old cause men and women to be filled with fear? Assuredly not! A poll was taken at a church forum in Florida during the winter season, when a large number of visitors were present. One of the questions was worded as follows: "Put a check mark beside the period which you regard as the happiest of your life. Childhood? Teens? Twenties? Thirties? Forties? Fifties? Sixties? Seventies?" It must have surprised the young people in the audience to learn that neither the teens nor the twenties were first choice.

"What is the happiest period of life" The sixties received the largest number of votes. Since the majority of the people present were in their sixties it was evident that they were answering the question by saying: "The best part of life is now!" They understood what Browning meant when he wrote:

> Grow old along with me!
> The best is yet to be,
> The last of life, for which the first was made:
> Our times are in His hand
> Who saith, "A whole I planned,
> Youth shows but half; trust God: see all, nor be afraid!"[1]

An unnumbered host of men and women have discovered that the second half of life is happier and more satisfying than the first. Many people look back on their youthful years as a time of strain. Satisfactions? Yes, but also frustrations and defeat. With the onset of the years they have gained a maturer judgment and an ability to get things accomplished. They have found loyal friends. The people in the community come not only to admire but to respect them. As individuals, and as members of society, they are more useful and honored at sixty-five than they were at twenty-five or thirty.

It is often true that women are more attractive as they

approach middle life. They lose some of the awkwardness and instability of youth. Broader experience develops an understanding of people which is reflected in their sympathies. That deeper sensitiveness to the needs of others becomes in time a part of their facial expression. They may have been quite plain-looking in their youth, but they take on a beauty with middle age. In every community we find people whose youthful behavior would need to be described as flighty, but who in their maturer years become delightful companions, possessing charming personalities.

The fear of growing old is part of the resistance to change which is characteristic of the life of most of us. But the latter half of life can be richer and fuller in meaning and happiness than the first if we gain the right perspective and the right approach is made.

Much of the common fear of old age is caused by the awareness that the latter years are sometimes accompanied by a physical and mental state which make it necessary for a person to be dependent on others for his care. The possibility of such a thing happening to them is enough to strike terror into their minds.

It is difficult to know how to allay this fear. Of course, there is the assurance that it will not happen in every case. Beyond that we know that the development of a wholesome attitude toward years of declining strength will help to keep the mind alert, and probably will have a part in keeping the body fit for the demands which may be made on it. For reasons beyond our control people do sometimes suffer from helpless old age, but often the period of vital health may be prolonged by maintaining a calm mind and an untroubled spirit. Even helplessness of body need not be dreaded when one has an outlook which captures and holds the admiration of those on whom we are dependent.

Let us examine the qualities and personality traits which can remove the fear of growing old. First, learn not to become irritated by little things. Young people are seldom troubled by this trait. Their natural physical stamina and buoyancy make it possible for them to accept criticism and disappointment without too great strain. They are not sufficiently set in their ways to make it impossible for them to change their plans when that is necessary. One of the first and surest signs of old age is the tendency to become irritated because little things are not exactly as you want them. When a man begins to fume and to fret because his slippers are not where he expects to find them, or when a woman, watching her daughter-in-law give the baby a sun bath, begins to criticize, saying, "We never did it that way," it is evident that they are growing old. They are irritated by little things.

Several hundred persons were waiting in Grand Central Station for the gate to open which would allow them to board their train. Everyone's interest was centered on a woman who rushed from one attendant to another asking if her train left from this or that gate. She paused only long enough to complain loudly that the station was too warm. She had arrived by taxi and, having considerable luggage, had employed two redcaps. When she arrived before the gate she discovered that some of the redcaps had carts to transport their luggage. The woman directed one of them to take all her luggage because she thought it would be less expensive. When the two who had brought her bags from the taxi insisted that they be paid for their services she flew into a rage. She roundly berated them. She attributed their request for pay to the fact that they were granted too much freedom by their union. After a lengthy discussion, the porters turned away. One of them said, "That old woman is the worst one I have ever met!" When he used the word "old" I turned to look at her. She was in her forties, but she was old because she could not accept the normal irritations of travel.

As habits of life become deeply set it is always difficult to alter the pattern. Older people are naturally more susceptible to the irritations which are felt when it is necessary to make changes. The struggle against the tendency to allow minor irritations to make life miserable must be made by everybody, whether young or old. But the older person has the bigger fight to win. His victory in this, however, will do a great deal toward maintaining a youthful spirit.

Next, keep alive an eagerness for new knowledge and experience. Many people are old before they are forty because they have stopped learning. They have the mistaken idea that their education was completed with high school or college. Since then they have read little or nothing except a newspaper or the current magazines.

I called to see a man in his late seventies who told me that he is specializing on Africa this year. He has read the life of David Livingstone, the books of Osa Johnson, Alan Paton's *Cry the Beloved Country,* and other books which deal with both the history and the present situation in Africa. His eyes light up when he imparts information or answers questions which demonstrate his new knowledge. He seems nearer thirty than he does eighty, for his mind is still young and vigorous.

Unlike the flesh, the spirit does not necessarily deteriorate with the years. Many of the happiest men and women in the world are those who are old in years but who are young in spirit. They have cultivated interests and activities which make their leisure a delight. They have not neglected the opportunity to read great books, to hear fine music, and to see the beauties of nature.

Never before in history has life been so interesting and varied as now. The music of the masters is available on records, in concerts, or through a selective use of radio. Libraries are stocked with books which reveal the life-beat of the ages. It is a tragedy that hundreds of the world's greatest books in any library are never taken from the shelves except during those weeks when classes in the public schools or colleges are searching for information to meet their assignments. These books are often lost to the public which is beyond high school age, but they offer adventure and romance for all those who will read them.

Hobbies which give us an opportunity to create and to build are invaluable. They have opened the windows of the mind for scores of those who had looked upon retirement as the end of life. One man has purchased an electric saw and lathe and has set up a workshop in his cellar. For forty years he had longed for such a place. Now he has time to enjoy it.

A busy workman used to sketch a bit in his spare moments. Now he has time to use this talent for landscape painting. The hours so spent bring great joy and satisfaction to him, as well as much pleasure to his family and friends.

Another man had always dreamed of settling down on a small farm. He purchased the land, built a log cabin with his own hands. Then, having bought a cow and some chickens, he started farming. Now he is enjoying in retirement the kind of life he had always wanted to live.

Retirement may mark the beginning of the best time of life for those who will continue to learn. Each day can be rich and full for one who is busy at creative tasks.

Occasionally we are thrilled by the example of someone who takes an active place of leadership in the community when he is well along in years. It was so when Winston Churchill, in his sixties, came back from retirement to rally his people against a foreign aggressor. Those who were privileged to know Bishop Edwin Holt Hughes of the Methodist Church, when he was in his eighties, were amazed at the vigor of his mind and spirit. His youthful enthusiasm brought joy and good fellowship wherever he went.

Edwin Markham published his "Eighty Poems at Eighty" at a time in life when most men are satisfied to rest on their laurels. People who knew Markham during those years will never forget the light in his eyes, or his zest for living. It was from the overflowing eagerness for life that he wrote in his eightieth year:

119

I laugh and lift hands to the years ahead!
"Come on: I am ready for you!"[2]

The youthful spirit is characterized by hope. Young people believe that tomorrow will see the realization of their ideals even if the present is dark and foreboding. For them the world is filled with adventure. Often they marry, or build or buy a home at a time when their elders assure them that this is not the proper period to be taking such a risk. Life is glorious with opportunity! They reach up bravely to accept it.

The transition from youth to age is accomplished when this spirit of hopeful anticipation changes first to calm acceptance of prevailing conditions, and then to the constant assertion that the world is going to pieces. Older people are naturally and properly more conservative, but the constant wailing that life was better in the yesterday has almost always proved a myth. For as long a time as men have lived on the earth some of the older generation have thought that the world was dying in their day.

With a fading confidence in civilization many have also lost faith in human beings. They have become convinced that the youth of today are evil in mind and without worthy purposes to guide them. They are certain that the deeds of young people are always leading them to destruction. They believe that this generation is not so spiritually minded as theirs, and is therefore in a hopeless condition.

Men and women who appear young at seventy have a different outlook. They have confidence in the wisdom and goodness of mankind. They glory in the frankness and idealism of youth. They look forward to the tomorrows with a wistful longing that they may have the opportunity to see the new inventions which will be made.

Fear of growing old will have little place in a life which is full of anticipation and hope for the future. To develop confidence in people and in the processes which make for advance is one of the best means of keeping the radiance of youth.

It is also important to keep busy helping people. Cynics sometimes scorn the activities of those who are sharing all they have with others. They wonder why it seems worthwhile. They do not realize that there are many compensations, but none more important than the invigorating power which comes when their personal problems shrink in size as their interest becomes centered in others who are in need. People who are busy helping to make a better community seem young and vital even if physically they may be somewhat infirm.

Many men and women have discovered that their advancing years have given them additional opportunities to share in community organizations and interests. Their mature judgment has made their leadership and counsel invaluable in activities which promote the welfare of children and youth. Such interests should be accepted as part of the normal responsibilities of those who have been blessed by living where conditions are favorable, but it serves also to cultivate the youthful spirit.

The way in which fear of old age is often dispelled by concern for the welfare of others was well illustrated by an incident found in Dr. Wilfred Grenfell's autobiography. He wrote:

In the early days of our mission among the Labrador fishermen someone in England organized the Fisher Lads' Writing Association. Each member took the names of so many orphan British boys at sea, and agreed to write them regularly. Sometimes these letters did more for those who wrote them than they did for those who received them. I remember in particular one elderly lady whose sole concern for years had been her own feelings and the state of her own health. She had enjoyed semi-invalidism for so long that it seemed unlikely she would ever be a thoroughly normal person again. Through the constant use of refined stimulants she succeeded in postponing that final illness which would have been a merciful relief to her long-suffering family. Joining our Letter Writing Association did wonders for this woman. The doctors were forgotten, the stimulants tabooed, and one by one all the insignia of invalidism were banished. Best of all, this woman began to be an asset rather than a liability in her own home. One day I saw her at a British fishing port, surrounded by a bevy of blue-jerseyed lads just off shipboard. They were some of the sailors to whom she had been writing. In thinking and working for them she had literally saved herself.[3]

Some of the great truths which the ages have produced are so simple that men pass them by in the search for something which seems more profound. Jesus said that in order to inherit eternal life "thou shalt love thy neighbor as thyself." The eternal life begins here on earth. We inherit it, and we lose all fear of growing old when we love and serve others.

Finally, remember that the help of God is available for those who will accept it. The fear of growing old is in large measure a fear of life itself. Neither life nor death is intimidating to those who have accepted the Christian answer to human need.

All of us are subject to the natural weaknesses of the physical body. These increase with the years. But the Christian faith declares that we are guided and led by the power of God, and that His plan for our lives includes an immortal destiny. How can a soul grow old by living eighty years when it accepts the assurance of eternity as real?

Beyond the encouragement which comes from realizing that we possess an immortal soul there is the confidence which results from the discovery that God will give strength for every day's journey. His presence calms the sometimes misdirected enthusiasm of youth, and it quickens the tired and discouraged spirit of those who are older. No one will be concerned with the fear of growing old who seeks and finds each day the divine wisdom and power by which life is made triumphant.

XIII

Fear of Facing God

MILLIONS OF NEEDY INDIVIDUALS HAVE FOUND AN UNFAILING source of mental and physical health in their religion. Yet there are many others to whom a twisted form of faith has become a major cause of nervous disorder. Whenever this tragedy occurs it is because religion has been misunderstood, or its power to effect changes in personality has been dissipated.

From the point of view of practical Christianity there are two attitudes toward God which defeat the Christian cause and tend to deprive the individual of the benefits which faith offers. One is to be afraid of God; the other is to ignore religion and deny the need for faith in a Divine Being. Strangely enough, both of these stem from the same source. Both originate in fear. The individual who ignores the implications of religion frequently resorts to lame excuses to explain his neglect. He declares that he is as good as most church members, or he shrugs aside the implications of faith with the assertion that it is not practical or necessary. What he doesn't realize is that too often his scorn or neglect of religion is a cloak to hide the fear of not facing his obligations to God, or this fear that God may call him to account for his failure.

The organized church may not be necessary to abundant living, but religion is. It is basic to life. The entire history of mankind on the earth cries out the truth that men grope for God until they find Him.

Attempts to explain away religion as unessential usually indicate a fear of God, and of the obligations which faith in Him may impose. That fear is dangerous. It not only erects a barrier between the self and the possibility of receiving strength from a vital faith, but it encourages one to use the method of escape in order to avoid the issue. Often he thinks that if he ignores religion he will not be perplexed and troubled by the cries of suffering humanity and the submerged restlessness within his own soul.

A better way is to examine the reason why men fear God, and endeavor to discover the secret of that relationship between God and man which brings inner peace and the ability to meet any adversity with courage and serenity.

Most fear originates during childhood. It is so with the fear of God. The early years are the formative period when a countless host of men and women come to feel that God is harsh, cruel, and vindictive.

It is well to understand clearly the source of such an impression of the Divine. It comes, in the first place, from false concepts. A child sometimes pictures God as an old man with a long, white beard. He usually is seated on a throne, ready to listen to the charges against little boys and girls who have committed wrong. Such an idea of God helps to make Him an object of terror rather than of respect or love.

Parents sometimes inadvertently contribute to this terrifying picture when they endeavor to frighten their children into obedience by the assertion that God is watching them.

A high-school student was attempting to explain the origin of the horror he felt when he thought of God. He said that as a child he had the habit of biting his finger nails. His mother had tried without success to correct him. Finally, she began to impress on him that God was watching him. "When she put me to bed at night," the youth explained, "my mother would warn me against biting my nails

124

by saying that God would be keeping an eye on me every minute, even when the lights were out, and would be very angry if I disobeyed. She did not tell me what punishment God would mete out, but I had pictures in my mind of a flaming hell."

The fear of God, which deprives a countless host of people of the peace and power which come with religious faith, has its origin in such distortions of the truth. The mind of the child is impressionable. It thinks in terms of fairies or ghosts almost as easily as of things that are real. Every mention of God to the child should be couched in words which will not sacrifice the concept of His personal interest and love to the idea of His greatness and majesty.

One who is aware that his thoughts of God cause him to grow tense with fear, or to have unpleasant feelings of helplessness, or an urgent desire to escape, needs to carefully analyze his experience to discover whether he is heir to a false conception of God accepted during his childhood years. He does not need to look only for specific teachings which were the cause of such feelings. Many of the distorted ideas of God are the result of the child's groping desire to give flesh and bones to thoughts which seemed mysterious.

However, the false concepts of God which cause fear are not limited to early years. Many adults are afraid of God because their associations with religion and with the idea of a Divine Being have been unpleasant. Two people came into our consultation room within a single morning to ask for help with their problems of faith. One was a skilled private secretary, and the other a successful business man. Both declared that the idea of God was unpleasant to them. "I never wanted to attend church, because every mention of God was turned into an attempt to stir the emotions," said the secretary. The business man declared that he had decided as a young man never again to step inside a church

125

as long as he lived, because "the God I heard about there didn't belong in my world. He was cruel, vindictive, and menacing. I've been afraid of Him ever since."

These two cases are typical of the experience of many people who are afraid of God because their ideas of His nature and of His relationship to their lives are out of keeping with the teachings of the Master.

Faith in God's dependability is fundamental to a well-adjusted life. To deny that He can be relied upon is to make room for the most dangerous type of fear. If the laws of the universe are subject to change at a moment's notice—either to bring favorable conditions to the good people, or misery and grief to the wicked—a condition of uneasiness is apt to remain in the mind. Fear becomes a ready ally to such thoughts. The fear-stricken man stands always on shifting sands. He has no rock on which he can build his life. He becomes afraid.

On the other hand, if a person has faith in the God whose nature never changes, whose rules are fixed and dependable, he has a sense of security even when factors in his environment tend to make him tremble.

The world gives us ample evidence that God is dependable. The scientists of this generation are making calculations which will cause the astronomers of a thousand years from now to turn their telescopes to the skies on a certain day at a certain minute to see a planet sailing into view. God's universe is dependable. Even the tragedies of fire and flood are a result of the laws of nature by which God governs the universe. If He were to change slightly his formulas for cause and result to make it impossible for a forest fire to sweep over a mountain it is probable that the orderliness of the universe would be disturbed in such a way as to cause greater catastrophes. If God were to change His laws of nature to prevent floods, it is probable that man would be encouraged in his waste of the forests, and thus cause further discord in the regular plan of life.

126

Our world is governed by principles of cause and effect, of system and order. Such chaos as we find can be remedied when men become aware of God and are willing to work with Him. But consider this, every denial of God's dependability throws the doubter back on a universe which is subject to whims and chance. Then he becomes afraid— afraid of the world, and afraid of the God who created it.

There is another source of man's fear. A consciousness of evil deeds committed, or opportunities lost, frequently makes God an object of terror. Immanuel Kant was impressed by the "moral law" in the universe. So, too, are millions of other men who are versed in neither philosophy nor theology. The challenge of right and wrong thrusts itself continually into the human situation. God, who is identified with that which is good, must inevitably inspire awe in those who allow themselves to think and do that which is evil. It is not to be wondered at that they are afraid when they have denied Him, or have broken His laws.

It is said of Moses that "he hid his face for he was afraid to look upon God." Men and women far less versed in religious truth, and less noble in their motives, have had a like fear. To rid the mind of that dark shadow is to learn one of the secrets of abundant living. Fear not only tramples peace and assurance into the dust, but it deprives its victims of the benefits of faith. It robs them of the power which is available to those who become aware of God and live by His truth.

In meeting and conquering this fear there are several principles which will prove helpful. They are designed to banish the fear by utilizing the possibilities of the Christian faith.

First, admit your need for God. The tragedy of mental and physical breakdown often follows a futile attempt to carry the responsibility of life alone. The boast of strength sufficient to carry the load unaided by divine resources makes an understanding of God difficult.

127

Admiral Byrd spent five months in a hut buried underneath an ice cap in the Antarctic. During that period he became desperately aware of his helplessness. He found that he was slowly being poisoned by carbon monoxide gas. The nearest help was more than a hundred miles away, shut off by an impassable wall of snow. He was unable to sleep; he became so feeble that he could not leave his bunk. Yet he felt that the power which saved his life was the result of an awareness of his need. He cried out for divine help. Later he wrote in his dairy, "I am not alone." This explains how he was able to carry on.

So the first step in realizing such an assurance is to admit the need for it. An arrogant spirit defeats any possibility that you may have the experience of divine help. It leaves fear untouched, forgotten perhaps in the moments when life is comfortable and satisfying, but a source of agonizing terror when self-sufficiency no longer is enough to enable you to bear up in some hour of trial.

Second, lift your knowledge of God to the highest levels. Too many of us are satisfied with interpretations of the Creator which do not represent the noblest knowledge which is available. Those who study the Salem witchcraft trials in early Massachusetts are bewildered to explain how the leaders of the colony held such a warped conception of God that it allowed them to indulge in such barbaric acts. The only explanation is that they held a false idea of truth, which was a product on the one hand of their own distorted view of life, and on the other of a false interpretation of religion.

People are seldom victims of a fear of God when their knowledge of Him is gained through a study of the words and acts of Jesus. One of His followers said to Him, "Show us the Father and it sufficeth us." Jesus answered, "Have I been so long time with you, and yet thou hast not known me? He that hath seen me hath seen the Father."[1]

What is God like when seen through the eyes of such a

witness? First, He loves people, all people. Second, He understands individual needs, and is sympathetic toward those who are suffering. Third, He is forgiving toward those who are repentant of evil. Fourth, He is harsh only to those who are hypocrites, bigots, or are motivated by greed or hatred. Jesus gives us a picture of the God who is worthy of respect and love. To know Him is to fear evil but to love Him as a Heavenly Father. It is a faith built on the noblest witness which has ever been given to a needy humanity.

Some seekers for truth find difficulty in associating the qualities of the Christ who lived at a certain period in time, and in the little country of Palestine, with the Eternal God who is the Creator of all the universe. For them there are other doorways open by which they may come to understand His nature and His works. These other means are not as direct, and millions of Christians would testify that they are not as satisfying, but the doorways are there. For one thing, they can learn to appreciate the natural law in the universe which must inevitably demand a lawgiver to explain it. They can gain a perspective of eternal beauty through the glory of the flowers, the trees, the mountains, and the sea. All of these demand a Creator to explain them. Or they can listen to the voice of the Eternal God through the medium of great music.

The possibilities of discovering a vital faith are manifold. God has not left us without a witness of His presence. It is a knowledge which will satisfy the needs of those who seek him. He will appear in such a nature as to be worthy of being worshiped, loved and honored. Such fear as remains is never caused by our idea of God, but by the awareness that we have not measured up to the opportunities which have been entrusted to us.

Third, keep your life a unity if you desire to avoid fear. It is impossible to live a hectic, disordered, worried life and, at the same time, hold fast to the concept of a loving God. A sophomore in college came to talk with me about his doubts. He felt that his religion had been undermined by the knowledge he had gained during his first year in college. In response to questions, he talked about his personal interests and of his part in campus life. When we came back to a discussion of his religion, he said, "I tell you I'm confused about my faith in God."

"Have you stopped to consider that you are confused about many things?" I replied. "You say you are in love with three young women, and cannot decide on a favorite. You are confused about your future career. You are confused about the choices which you must make of studies, companions, and social habits. It seems to me that you are confused about all of life. Perhaps your religious faith will be more satisfying if you will order your thinking and actions around a central purpose and goal."

Every individual who desires to know God is faced with a similar need. It is always difficult to maintain a close fellowship with a Divine Friend if broad areas in the personality are in conflict. Family tensions inevitably react on religious faith. A young man who feels lost in his occupational interests almost always feels lost in his relationships with God.

These lesser matters can be handled with a hope of success if the seeker has first gained a knowledge of, and a fellowship with, God.

It is essential for vital faith to see life as a unity. Without it the individual tends to have a distorted idea of God and an outlook on the future in which there is little assurance of peace. Center your life around the highest goals and purposes that you know. Then you will discover that your fear of the Divine has been forgotten before the knowledge of His majesty and of His personal interest in each one who seeks Him.

Fourth, follow the practices which help to make God seem real. Foremost of these is the habit of public worship. Attend church services regularly. The mere attendance at the service is not enough, of course. Church worship offers no guarantee that God will become a vital factor in daily living. People can attend church and still be as far from God as the East is from the West. But a wise use of the privilege of worship insures any seeker of an opportunity to know more about Him. The customary rituals which are followed in church services have been tested in the crucible of human experience for many generations. They contain the essential elements to heal the wounds of doubt and to give a therapeutic aid by establishing faith.

Meditation on the passages in the Bible which throb with the assurance of the Divine Presence is another of the habits which provide a spiritual medicine to destroy the germs of fear. Prayer is also an effective agent for such healing.

God will always seem a part of the mystery of the universe. Because of that fact, it is a temptation to halt in the quest to know Him before you have reached the place where fear can be banished. Yet habits of meditation and worship enable eager seekers to find the secret of triumphant living.

If we are to win the victory of faith over fear, we must examine carefully our attitudes toward religion and life. Unfortunate personal relationships, and a distorted type of religion, have contributed to give many of us a concept of God which cannot pass the simplest test of faith as expressed in the life of Jesus Christ. Adventure forth in the quest for an understanding of God which will be full and satisfying. The pilgrimage will enrich your life, and will remove forever your fear of God.

XIV

Fear of Sickness

FEAR OF SICKNESS HAS HAUNTED MEN SINCE THE BEGINNING OF recorded history. The medicine man was second in importance to the chief in ancient tribes because he claimed to have power over sickness and death. He employed fear as a means to control the people. Fear of sickness became the horror which pursued them from childhood to the end of their lives.

Feelings of terror caused by sickness remained even after advancing culture had pushed the medicine man out of the life of the community. No amount of knowledge could banish the gnawing fear of being ill. Because the Christian Church taught men to have faith in a God who was all-powerful, they often looked to religion to remove this fear by providing a spring of healing. The shrines at Lourdes, St. Anne de Beaupré, and other places in the world, are an evidence of the fact that people insist that there is a close connection between religion and health. The existence of the healing sects further indicates the human longing to find a means to avoid the pains of the body, as well as the pains of the mind which inevitably accompany them.

The close connection between Christianity and healing had its origin in the miracles of Jesus. Jesus healed the sick. His ministry was divided between healing and teaching. Yet we often miss the fact that on many occasions He declared that fear was the cause of the sickness. He insisted that fear must be replaced by faith before the healing miracle could be performed. Indeed, in the words of many of the miracles, His work was finished when the fear had been rooted out. Fear was the major enemy. The battle line was established by faith to halt the incessant attacks of this grim destroyer of happiness.

Most Christians accept and utilize the advances in modern medicine and surgery as part of the providence of God to insure a longer and healthier life. Yet the fears of sickness have not been lessened. One of the country's leading physicians, referring to the large number of cases of cancer which do not come to the attention of doctors until they are in an advanced stage, said: "We would go a long distance toward the cure of cancer if we could find a way to get rid of the fear of it.

Fear of sickness ruins many lives. I went into a home which is made nearly ideal by the happy relationship between the parents and children. The mother is active in church and community interests. She is popular with a large circle of friends. But the home was turned into a place of tension when the mother was informed that it would be necessary for her to go to the hospital for surgical treatment. The operation was not serious, but she was certain that her doctor was deceiving her, and that death would be the probable result. Fear of sickness turned her into an entirely different person. She withdrew from the interests which had previously meant so much to her. She could not care adequately for her family. Her children were puzzled to know what had changed their mother from a happy, gay person into one who was continually weeping. They did not understand it, but the villian was fear.

Fear does not always appear on the surface. The personality is healthier if it does. Sometimes the fear of sickness is hidden even from those who are closest to its victim. It does its work at night when, tossing sleeplessly, a man worries about what to do, what doctor to see, or when the disease will become serious. Even as he does his work he thinks continually about the possible consequences of his threatened illness. A party or an outing with friends is marred by thoughts of imminent disaster. He builds up shadowy distortions on the meager foundation of a tiny lump or a lingering sore. A sharp pain, or a shortness of breath, is all he needs to be certain that catastrophe is close at hand. When he actually becomes ill, or when he is a patient in a hospital, the fear is more intense. He imagines every discomfort is a prelude to a final illness. Fear warps his vision and colors his perspective.

Everyone is at times a victim of such fears. Those who have never experienced that kind of agony of mind belong in a narrow and charmed circle. Most of us need to face the issue, and discover how we can avoid such pitfalls.

There are certain habits of mind which can help to lift the burden of sickness. The cultivation of these attitudes will serve us when we are afraid that sickness may come, or during the more difficult periods when we are actually ill.

It always helps if we are willing to face the facts. Fear seldom flourishes in the presence of knowledge. It is usually true that the more a patient knows, the less he fears. That does not mean that the illness may not be serious. Perhaps the slow progress of disease indicates that the end of life is not far distant. Whatever the case may be, the mind suffers less if the forebodings are brought into the open, and the truth becomes known.

Such a facing of the facts will often make the fears seem a foolish sign of weakness. What seemed an indication of serious illness may prove to be merely a natural development of the years, or a temporary condition brought on by overwork or overeating.

A businessman was obsessed by the fear that he was losing his hearing. To his family and his business associates it was evident that he was becoming deaf. He refused to see a doctor because he feared that a hearing aid would be prescribed. For two years he struggled against the cloud of silence which gathered about him. Every appeal that he see a doctor was answered by a curt refusal. He even resorted to the practice of carrying on conversations in writing in order to avoid the struggle to hear. It was only when he was forced to make a choice between seeking medical advice or giving up his position that he decided to see a physician. The physician made a careful examination and then gave the astounding diagnosis that there was nothing wrong with his ears except that they were stopped up. A week of treatments and his hearing was completely restored. The man's fear had caused him unmeasured misery. His life for two years could have been free of anxiety if he had been willing to admit his infirmity and seek a cure.

Even if the grim reality indicates serious or fatal illness it is better to meet the actual situation openly. The mind can busy itself with necessary adjustments to any handicap if its strength is not dissipated in the possibilities of what *might* be.

Few people can boast of perfect health. Nearly everyone has some weakness of the body. Even in this generation when the fight against disease has enabled us to anticipate longer life there are constant threats to health. Indeed, because we have become conscious of the possibilities of infection, we are more sensitive than people formerly were to slight illnesses. We know that a mild pain is in some instances the forerunner of appendicitis, a slight sore throat is sometimes the first stage of diphtheria or infantile paralysis. Fear has little power to harm those who willingly accept the weaknesses of the body, looking directly into the actual condition, and constantly resisting the temptation to be stampeded into terror by symptoms which may not be serious.

When illness threatens to put a permanent limit on activity the resultant damage to the system by fear can be avoided if the situation is faced realistically, and necessary adjustments made. Luther Burbank, as a young man, was a semi-invalid. For several years he was troubled by a fear that he could not make a go of life. He felt that he was doomed to an early death. Finally, as a drastic measure, he determined to change his occupation. He left the hot, dusty factory in Worcester, Massachusetts, where he was working, and secured employment in a plant nursery. Though his condition improved by outdoor labor, the long New England winters further weakened his bodily strength. Again he decided on a drastic move as a means to conquer both his physical weakness and the fears which accompanied them. He moved to California in the hope that the warmer climate would prove beneficial. In time he recovered his health and achieved a success which placed him in the forefront of America's greatest naturalists.

Many normal and happy people have had to coax their bodies through long years of weakness. A heart ailment sometimes has made it necessary to curtail work and pleasure, and yet has still allowed its victim to enjoy real success and happiness. A life which was marked by less activity, and systematic periods of rest, often has proved more satisfying than the hurry of former days. A man who, because of a heart attack, was forced to make a drastic restriction in his pursuit of business and social life, declared: "I have spent more evenings at home during this past six months than in all the twenty years previous to my illness. And I like it. I have learned again to read. I think I enjoy my family, also, more than I ever did before."

Fear will have little power to disturb one who is willing to face up to reality. Some of the fears will prove groundless, and the sharp edge of the others will be blunted when we learn to accept the limitations which our weakness imposes on us.

In the second place, look forward eagerly to the ways in which the experience of sickness will enrich your life. Many who have suffered from a long illness have testified to the fact that it was during their hours of suffering that they found the divine power by which life was made more abundant.

You have probably met a woman for whom a hospital experience was the greatest single adventure in her life. As long as she lives she will find pleasure in relating the intimate details of the operating room, the doctor's skill, and the nurses' kindness. She delights in the opportunity to become well enough acquainted with a stranger to be able to say, "That reminds me of the time when I was in the hospital. . . ." Then she launches into the tale which has become wearisome to her friends, but which for her never grows old. It was the high moment in her life!

More richly blessed is the person who, during his "horizontal holiday," realizes anew the importance of those things which have eternal worth. Periods spent in a hospital often give a unique opportunity to rediscover neglected values. Friendship becomes precious. The flowers, and cards, and visitors indicate that there are many people who have a real concern for his welfare. That makes life seem worth while. It is easy to slip into the assumption that people in general are selfish and greedy. It is not hard to decide that neighborliness has become a lost art in American life. But in the hour of sickness we may learn, as many others have learned, that we are appreciated and loved, that there are those who are glad and willing to take time from their busy lives to think about our needs.

Sickness often is the means by which men recover values which have been temporarily lost. The director of a large business had come to the end of a hospital experience. He had undergone a serious operation, and had for a time been critically ill. Previous to his illness he had shown little concern for the welfare of his church and community. Such interest as he did manifest was limited to an occasional gift of money. On the day before he left the hospital he talked to his pastor about the change which had come in his thinking:

137

"I have discovered that many things are important to me which, for a long time, I haven't done anything about," he said. "Somehow, goodness and kindness and faith have taken on a new significance. I want to get back into the church, and do my full share in promoting its program. It isn't that I'm afraid to die—or anything like that—it's just that I have found out that certain values which I have neglected for a long time are now important to me."

Many other men and women have recovered lost ideals and faith through the experience of sickness. On their recovery they have started to live more fully than they ever had lived before.

Often sickness contributes the inspiration for a more abundant life. As the result of contact with sickness in his home Charles Mayo decided as a youth to study medicine. A. J. Cronin was a successful medical practitioner in London until a physical breakdown forced him to give up his practice and go to the country for a long period of recuperation. Abject despair was his first reaction to the illness. He was cut off from income, as well as from the profession to which he had given the best years of his life. In that hour he turned to writing to give an outlet to his pent-up feelings. He produced *The Citadel,* and by that novel was launched on a writing career which has gained him a place among the foremost authors of this generation. If he had not been burdened by illness he probably never would have become a writer, and the world would have missed the inspiration of his pen.

The fear of sickness will be less of a threat to contentment if we approach the experience expecting that worthy values will develop out of the hardship. Beyond our ability to measure the result at the time when pain seems so devastating, we will find in sickness the key to a full and abundant life.

Sometimes the destructive influence of sickness is limited if an individual will keep busy, turning his attention to new interests, or to the opportunities which come to him to serve others. Most of us have discovered that a headache often seems less severe if we decide to go about our work, or to the regular responsibilities of the day, rather than to pamper ourselves. Keeping busy distracts our attention from our pains, and leaves no room for the fears which constantly absorb our waking thoughts.

When sickness threatens to keep one bedfast, or at least partially disabled for a long period, there is healing power for the mind in doing something constructive or helpful. Robert Louis Stevenson must have been tempted to stay in bed every day during the last three years of his life. His body was burned by fever. He found relief for the pain, and prolonged his life, by writing books of adventure and poems to delight children. Because of his courageous action he discovered that fear had no hold on him.

But the best and most certain way to rid the mind of fear comes to those who regularly practice the presence of God. Sarah Williams, in "The Old Astronomer" declared:

> Though my soul may set in darkness, it will
> rise to perfect light,
> I have loved the stars too fondly to be
> fearful of the night.[1]

The darkness of fear can be dispelled for those who learn to make practical use of the assurances of religion. Faith in God restores confidence in the ultimate goodness of the universe. It places the seal of importance on human personality. It offers daily help and strength, by which pain and physical weakness may be accepted and often overcome. It gives the hope of healing; or, if healing cannot be anticipated in the way and at the time we desire, it gives the power to endure the pain.

Alice Bretz is one of many victims of illness who have demonstrated that the rich promises of the Christian faith are real. She was a happy, normal housewife until the day

139

when a haze began to develop over her eyes. The shadows grew darker until there was no difference between night and day. She was blind.

She thought at first that the handicap was only temporary. When she went to a hospital for an operation it was with confidence that she would recover her sight. There came a day, however, when her doctor stood at her bedside and said, "I am sorry to tell you that you are blind. You will never see again."

In the moments which followed she was a victim of the fear which has marred and weakened the sick and maimed of every age. She recoiled from a growing horror of life as she must face it.

She was called back to the realities of her situation by the words of a clergyman who came into the room. Putting his hand over her eyes he said, "God has laid His cross on you, my child."

Mrs. Bretz lay silent. She declared that she could feel a heavy, cruel cross crushing her. She was weighed down by it. Then she remembered the church where as a girl she was confirmed. She recalled how the sanctuary looked on a Sunday morning when sunshine streamed through the beautiful, stained-glass windows. She could see the sunlight falling on the gold of the cross, making it gleam as it passed in the processional. She could hear the hymn which the choir sang when they entered the sanctuary:

> Onward, Christian soldiers
> Marching as to war,
> With the cross of Jesus
> Going on before.

Suddenly the truth burst on her fear-darkened soul that the cross always goes on before. It leaves no room for fear of life and its burdens. The cross is a symbol of victory. "Though I must be blind all my days," she cried, "I will turn my cross into victory and let it lead me as a singing soul. I will not be defeated."[2]

That is the response of faith to the fear of sickness. Defeat is turned into victory. Yet the process is seldom as instantaneous as the expressed desire for it. We do not merely wish for faith. Almost always it is gained through a willing surrender of self to divine purposes, or through the practice of the presence of God.

Mrs. Bretz was able to realize the divine presence by a wise use of memory. She recaptured the holy experiences of her youth, and utilized them to meet her pressing needs. Such a practice of the presence of God is often rewarding. The rich stores of memory frequently can be drawn on to recover the treasures of faith. But there are other ways by which they can be re-established. Attendance at services of worship often helps to unlock the reservoir. Sometimes daily meditation and prayer are the best means of putting us in tune with the eternal.

Whatever the method utilized, it is essential to seek God and to learn the secret of the power which is available through faith.

The effectiveness of many individuals is constantly limited by a fear of sickness. It follows them wherever they go. It distorts their outlook, and turns them into weaklings. No life can be complete and full until this fear is overcome. Yet there is reason to have confidence. The mind need not be blighted by this obsession. There is release for all those who are willing to utilize a practical and effective plan for abundant living. Disease and infirmities may remain to hamper the physical body, but fear of sickness can always be dispelled by a living faith.

141

XV

Fear of Death

MANY PEOPLE ARE BEWILDERED, AND SOMETIMES MADE ashamed, by the feelings of terror which pursue them whenever they face the fact that their physical life has an inevitable end.

Such fears have always been a part of human experience. Death has seemed a dark shadow to men of every age. That is not strange, for associations with death are often depressing. It marks the end of earthly things, the breaking of precious human ties.

The customs which are followed at the time of a person's decease, the public mourning, and the ritual at the grave, contribute to the feeling of strangeness and solemnity. Grief and agony of mind are frequently a real factor, also. All of this tends to make the termination of physical life an experience which men strive desperately to escape. As this is impossible, they are haunted by the fears of facing death.

Even in the earliest civilizations there is evidence that people were victimized by fear. The long and tedious preparations which the Egyptians made before they interred the bodies of their dead indicate that they had a persistent fear of the unknown and a desire to preserve the appearance of the physical life.

The ancient Persian civilization was characterized by progress in architecture, painting, and human relationships over any civilization which preceded it. Yet archeological discoveries and remnants of their art demonstrate clearly that they were victims of this fear. It was so pronounced that all those who even touched a dead body were penalized by society. Men who were appointed to the task of disposing of the dead were required to undergo rites of purification before they could return to normal society.

In every age common people and royalty share alike this very real fear of death. Queen Elizabeth of England came to the end of her long reign with almost the entire world acclaiming her. Her sense of justice and her encouragement of many movements which made for human progress had earned the lasting devotion of her people. Yet she was unable to escape the universal terror which so often blights the mind at the hour of death. "I would give all my possessions for one moment of time," she is reported to have cried during her last illness. It is evident that she, the great queen, was as much afraid as any of her humble subjects.

Thomas Hobbs earned a place of deserved recognition among the world's foremost philosophers. He thought deeply concerning life and its meaning. Yet when he faced death, he cried: "I'm taking a fearful leap in the dark." He was a victim of the fear which has disturbed men in every century.

Dr. Samuel Johnson was quoted by his friend Boswell as declaring that "if one were to think constantly of death, the business of life would stand still." Johnson and Boswell endeavored to avoid discussions of the subject. Both were haunted by fear, the reason differing with the character of the men. Johnson feared death because he thought it meant the beginning of judgment for his soul. Boswell's attitude was shaped by his conviction that death marked the end of everything for the individual.

During the Middle Ages, the Inquisition, the black plague, and the prevailing attitude of carelessness toward life contributed to build up an ever-present fear of death. It was during that period that the skull and cross-bones came into general use. They were carved on the abutments of

143

bridges, on drinking-cups, rings, and china as a constant reminder that life was fleeting. This practice was meant to stimulate fear, and it succeeded in accomplishing that end. Men were terrified by death.

Evidence indicates that this fear is an outgrowth of the customary attitudes which we assume and practice. We tend to fear the unknown, the painful, and the unpleasant. For many people death is a venture into a realm beyond their understanding, a realm which is frightening. Even the efficient services of a modern funeral home cannot cover the stark fears which begin when a child first sees a funeral procession moving slowly down a street, or when he is confronted by the death of someone he knows. Death is symbolized by tears, black clothes, and a black hearse. It means uncertainty and separation. It makes him afraid.

Almost everyone is gripped by fear until he consciously accepts a faith which has enough power to banish it. Other fears can be conquered by the application of secular ideas, but the terror of death needs spiritual light before its shadows can be dispelled.

The kind of faith which gives an answer is not limited merely to the presentation of the idea of immortality. That is important. But a faith which lifts the burden of fear must be able to make life every day an experience in abundant living. Brooding thoughts of death have little room in the mind of one whose years are made rich by happy human relationships. Michael de Montaigne had that in mind when he said, "He who would teach men to die must teach them to live."

A group of women were discussing the unexpected passing of a dear friend. Their conversation left no doubt that they looked on death as a fearful experience. One of the women said, "I try never to talk about it." Her remark evidently expressed the sentiments of the others. They mentioned the fact that the end of life often comes quite unex-

144

pectedly. Then one of the group tried to explain why death seemed so terrifying. "Death is so—so—final," she said.

The end of life always seems final to those who have built their major interests around material and physical things. When clothes, and money, and social approval are accepted as our supreme values we must inevitably find death to be the absolute end.

But the experience is different for those who are motivated by a higher ideal and purpose. They find joy in living. Every day is a challenge to service. They carry the burden of those who are in need. They are not shaken by the thought of death because the major interest in their life is unbroken. The results of kindly service remain after death has done its worst.

Those who live by such an ideal are never obsessed by the feeling that death will sweep away everything for which they have striven. They have neither the time nor the inclination to think morbidly about the end of life, but if they do think about it, it is without the emptiness of hope which stirs fear in the minds of those whose outlook is purely materialistic.

Keep life rich and abundant. That is important even when one retires from an occupation which has absorbed his interest and strength during his working years. Make every day an adventure. This does not need to be physically taxing. It may be the discovery of a new satisfaction in the pages of a book. It may result from a conversation with a neighbor or an acquaintance who is longing for encouragement. It may occur through the writing of a letter, or through helping a garden to blossom where the ground seems dead or choked with weeds.

A woman who was victimized by fears of sickness and death came to ask for spiritual help. In the conversation about the factors which caused her anxieties I inquired about her family background. She said that her father had been the happiest person she had ever known. He had lived to be eighty-four years old, and had never experienced a serious illness. When I inquired if she could explain why her father was such a happy man she made no reply. The question seemed to require consideration. "During his last ten years he was happy because he had his family, his friends, and his garden," she said at last. "He seemed to keep on living so he could see his flowers bloom, or his grandchildren graduate from school. He always had something ahead to which he could look forward."

Death has no power to strike fear into the mind of such a man. His life is too full of experiences which are a part of the eternal plan which unfolds year by year.

Montaigne was speaking with a wisdom which answers the needs of people in every age when he counseled those who seek to prepare men to die to "teach them to live." That approach to life is the first key to unlock the prison-house of fear. An abundance of love and kindliness and interest in people give death the rôle of a stranger who is powerless to make us afraid.

The second segment in the triangle of ideas which overcomes the fear of death is the discovery and acceptance of the concept that there is intelligence and meaning in the universe.

Charles Darwin shook the self-satisfied world of the nineteenth century by the publication of his *Origin of the Species*. In their harangues of protest against Darwin's work his critics failed to appreciate the fact that he had laid the foundation for a concept of a universe which is orderly and meaningful. It was not Darwin's purpose to discuss religion, but the picture of the world which he presented could not be explained without a Creator. Because his world was orderly and purposeful, Charles Darwin found it easy to accept death. He declared that he was not in the least afraid to die. He had courage rather than triumph, but even this effectively banished fear when the end seemed at hand.

146

During the Victorian age in England people were absorbed with the idea of death. Long deathbed scenes were frequently incorporated into their literature. Triumphant words in the last moments of life were seized upon to give encouragement to those with less faith or greater fear. Emily Brontë expressed her confidence in God's continuing purposes in a poem which she wrote near the end of her life:

> No coward soul is mine,
> No trembler in the world's storm-troubled sphere:
> I see Heaven's glories shine,
> And faith shines equal, arming me from fear.
>
> With wide-embracing love
> Thy spirit animates the years,
> Pervades and broods above,
> Changes, sustains, dissolves, creates, and rears.
>
> Though earth and moons are gone,
> And suns and universes ceased to be,
> And Thou wert left alone,
> Every existence would exist in Thee.
>
> There is no room for Death,
> Nor atom of his might could render void:
> *Thou—Thou art being and breath,*
> And what Thou art may never be destroyed.[1]

Such words make it understandable why Emily Brontë was unafraid to face death. During her last weeks her body was wracked by pain. She had contracted a severe cold at the funeral of her brother Bramwell. When death came she raised herself from her rocking chair to a standing position. No blind terror dismayed her. Her lifelong confidence in the continuing purposes of a Divine Creator gave her strength for every need.

Fear of death is powerless to disturb those who recognize that there is meaning in the human struggle. Christians always have lived triumphantly when they were aware that their efforts and sacrifices were contributing to the realization of the Kingdom of God. They saw themselves as sharers in an unfolding plan. The plan had an earthly practicality, but it had a heavenly goal. Death could not halt it. Instead, death often became the means by which the dream could be more fully realized.

Death will always seem a stark tragedy, an end of all striving, if life has no purpose to explain and justify it. But the acceptance of the basic Christian concept of the providence of God will change all of that. It will and does make life worth living. Every shadow of fear is removed when each human act is seen as a part of the eternal plan.

A triumphant faith in personal immortality is the third side in the triangle of ideas which lifts this burden of fear. Other suggestions serve to stimulate courage, but immortality makes death an introduction to a better and fuller life.

Isaac Watts voiced the faith which has satisfied the needs of many Christians:

> When I can read my title clear
> To mansions in the skies,
> I'll bid farewell to every fear,
> And wipe my weeping eyes.[2]

When we attempt to analyze the fact that the idea of immortality changes our attitude toward death we find help in discovering that certain men in every age gave us vivid examples of the triumph of faith. John of the Cross, a mystic of the Middle Ages, was told by his physicians that he had only a few hours to live. His faith had, for many years, made heaven seem real. He had written with confidence concerning immortality. When death was at hand he is quoted as saying: "I was glad when they said to me, 'We will go into the house of the Lord.' Since hearing those glad tidings, I have felt no pain whatsoever."

Death was not a dread experience for this aged saint.

148

Instead, it was an open door from the earthly life into the heavenly. He was eager and willing to begin the journey.

Nor does the evidence concerning immortality originate only in the religious leaders and mystics. George Herbert had thought so profoundly about heaven that he was happy to face death. He was a practical man of the world who won honors on the field of battle by his bravery and his skill. One day "he changed his sword and silk clothes for a canonical habit" and lived the rest of his life—only four years—as the parish minister at Bremerton in England. During that period he seemed to dwell in two worlds. He had an abounding appreciation for the beauties of the earth. His poetry, and sermons, and ministry of kindness enriched a multitude of lives. Yet he seemed also to have claimed a residence in heaven. Perhaps it was his painful illness which encouraged those thoughts. George Herbert knew no fear of death, because he expected it to mark the beginning of a continuing life which would be satisfying and full. His biographer says of him that he sang on his deathbed "such hymns and anthems as the angels and he now sing in heaven."

Not many practicing Christians experience during their lifetime so complete an identification with an immortal city. But every follower of Jesus can know something of that certainty. The faith promises it. The witness of the ages encourages it. The personal experience of a man or a women with God through prayer and fellowship gives unmistakable hints of it.

Cultivate the awareness of immortality by steeping your mind in the promises which religion offers. Seek also the witness of the poets, the philosophers, the theologians, and the saints who testify to their confidence in immortality. Such a practice will establish a strong foundation of assurance which will be impervious to fear.

Not only will the fear of death fall before the power of a positive affirmation concerning life, but every other fear will have less power to affect personal and social relationships adversely. If immortality is an assured fact, the sharp barbs of criticism, or of defeat, or of threatened sickness have less power over the personality. Immortality gives meaning to life for every person in every generation. It injects strength into lives which are crushed by disappointment or defeat. Any individual can bear with calm fortitude the hardships which circumstance or evil intentions have imposed on him if he has a confident assurance of immortality.

The disciples of Jesus of Nazareth scurried for shelter when their master was arrested, condemned, and crucified. They were afraid of persecution and the inevitable death which accompanied it. But after the resurrection they became changed men. Their fears of death were banished. They came to realize the significance of the words which Jesus had spoken. "I am the resurrection and the life," He had said. "He that believeth in me, though he were dead, yet shall he live."[3] At the time the words were uttered they seemed significant only to Mary and Martha of Bethany. After the resurrection they became meaningful for each of the disciples. The hope of immortality became a positive assurance. Fear no longer made them weaklings in the presence of opposition to the teachings of Jesus. They went out to live and to die for their faith.

Death has no terror for those who cultivate the Christian assurance of immortality. However, the best of its contribution to human poise is lost if its comfort is sought only in hours of bereavement. True, it serves well as a healing force for the spirit at a time when personal sorrow strikes hard. Yet it promises much more. It assures the seeker that he has an eternal destiny. It puts the seal of holiness on life every day. The common tasks are made to seem more sacred. All of life becomes rich in divine possibilities. The fear of death is forever banished from the mind.

XVI

Fear, Man's Servant or Tyrant

FEAR SOMETIMES SERVES A USEFUL PURPOSE. IT PROTECTS US from danger, and shields us from disaster. Often, however, it gets out of control. Then it becomes a cruel tyrant, driving us, lashing us, crippling our lives.

Humanity is plagued by many different types of fear: fear of the dark, of crowds, of being alone; fear of high places, or of closed places, or of wide open fields; fear of having children, of sickness, or of death; fears caused by a sense of guilt, resulting from deeds long since committed; fear of God—of denying and neglecting Him; fear of hell and of heaven. These, and countless others, prey on the minds and darken the lives of many, many people.

When fear strikes, definite changes take place in the physical body. Dr. George Crile observed the symptoms in animals at a time when they were stricken by sudden fear. He described what he saw in these words:

They may be likened to an automobile with the clutch thrown out but whose engine is racing at full speed. The gasoline is being consumed, and machinery is being worn, but the machine as a whole does not move, though the power of its engine may cause it to tremble.[1]

The reaction to fear in the human body is similar. The heart beats faster. Breathing is accelerated, and the glands are stimulated to greater activity. The muscles become taut, preparing for struggle or flight. A strain is placed on the whole physical system. The body tends to become worn and

151

tired. The possibility of a breakdown at some point is greatly increased.

The price which fear exacts from the mind and the body causes many individuals to evade every threat of fear as if it were a poison. Excessive fear is a poison, of that there is no doubt. But in an attempt to avoid exaggerated anxiety or terror we should not fail to recognize the indispensible part which fear plays in providing protection against dangerous or hostile forces.

Men never could have survived the changes which the ages have demanded without constructive fear. Fear warned the inhabitants of primitive civilizations of threats to their security. The battle against animals and natural elements in their environment could not have been won without the constant warnings which came to them by fear.

Shakespeare has Laertes remind Ophelia that "safety lies in fear." It is an observation which is valid in every age. Fear has always been a watchman for safety and security. The pride which men felt after fire and its uses had been discovered soon had to be tempered by fear of the consequences of flames which were uncontrolled. Without such warnings the earth might have been consumed in man's exaltation because he thought fire had become his servant.

Fear is an elemental alarm system. It is an indispensible part of our means of self-preservation. A fearless man would have difficulty remaining alive for a single day in the tangled confusion of traffic in any large metropolitan city.

During a summer weekend the radio stations of America co-operated with state safety councils in warning millions of motorists of the dangers of reckless driving. They repeated the same phrase again and again in spot announcements: "Don't GO through your windshield," they said. "LOOK through it." The appeal was to fear. Few drivers of automobiles have not been confronted in reality, or by photographs, with accidents in which a driver was hurled through the windshield of his car. The appeal to drive slowly was made by stimulating a fear of the consequences of a lack of care.

The United States Forestry Service has campaigned widely for the prevention of forest fires. It has made two basic appeals to the public. One of these attempts to stimulate a sense of obligation. People are asked to take precaution with fire as a part of their duty to their fellow citizens and to their country. The other appeal is through fear. Pictures are printed showing the red holocaust of forests in flame. The natural result of this publicity is to create fear. By making us terrified at the thought of fire the Forestry Service hopes to influence us to exercise greater care.

Fear serves us every day by its wise reminders of the consequences of carelessness. There are numerous gun accidents, but there would be more if fear had not influenced many men either to avoid entirely the use of firearms, or to exercise extreme caution in handling them. Fear saves the housewife from the possibility of a hundred serious accidents every day. The caution used in each act of housekeeping, from the use of a bread knife to handling a hot electric iron, is stimulated by a fear of the consequences of negligence.

The mechanical advances which have been made during the twentieth century have placed a countless number of dangerous devices at the disposal of man. Only a wise heeding of the warnings which are given through fear saves us from severe accidents or death.

The major airlines educate the public to the idea that commercial flying is comparatively safe. They endeavor to remove any natural fear of flying by listing the number of million passenger-miles which have been flown without accident. But the airlines demonstrate a wise use of fear by the elaborate precautions which they take to insure the safety of the passengers. Weather charts are studied, mechanical equipment and personnel are scrutinized. Even the most traveled air official has a reasonable amount of fear

153

when his life depends on the ability of a plane to remain aloft.

In every phase of our civilization there are mechanical servants of man which at times become a threat to security. Only a willing acceptance and wise use of the warnings which fear gives can save us from disaster. These warnings are a necessary and helpful servant of man.

Fear is not only indispensable to safety, but it is an essential element in contributing to human progress. The writer of the Book of Proverbs declared that "the fear of the Lord is the beginning of wisdom."[2] Fear often contributes to knowledge. But it does more than that. It is frequently a driving force which inspires men to remarkable achievements in their personal and social life.

Fear of disease is the greatest single factor which encourages medical progress. Tuberculosis was rampant throughout the world at the turn of the present century. It was the custom to speak of the disease in hushed tones. Many would not use the name, but made whispered references to T.B. Fear made tuberculosis seem the greatest scourge since the black plague. Yet out of that fear came a united effort to control and conquer this threatening menace. Money was forthcoming to build special hospitals and sanitoriums. Many doctors devoted their professional careers to research and study of the causes and cure. Once the fear began to seep relentlessly into the experience of a large percentage of the population, there was no hesitation in searching for a possible means to control this white ghost which might steal away their loved ones.

In the broader sense it can be said that fear of poverty was the primary drive which led to the establishment of industry. The creative urge was in some measure responsible, but more than anything else was the desire of men to avoid the specter of hunger and want.

Fear of ignorance prompted men to found schools and colleges. Men who had been deprived by poverty of education often became the benefactors of institutions of higher learning in their later lives.

Fear often inspires arduous and difficult efforts. Not only love, but fear, gives wings to the feet. No other single element in their experience explains the remarkable achievements of some men who were born in humble surroundings. Certainly, the desire for social recognition was a factor in a a large number of the cases in which men attained fame in music, literature, or business. The deep yearning for security was a driving force in many others. But a spur to most of their achievements was the fear which had gained a hold on their lives during childhood. That fear became a driving force which led them to work against handicaps to reach noble ends.

At the age of twelve, Michael Pupin came to America as an immigrant. Because he was penniless and without knowledge of any occupation by which he could support himself, the authorities at the port of entry questioned the wisdom of allowing him to enter New York. When he was finally permitted to leave the ship his entire resources totaled only five cents. He was in a strange country, and without money or friends. No wonder he was afraid! But that fear became the compulsion which shaped his life. It impelled him to accept the most menial kind of work. Out of it came a determination to study and strive unceasingly until he could attend college. It spurred him to remarkable achievements in science. Had he been comfortable and affluent he might never have made unceasing efforts to reach worthy goals. The power of fear was a wholesome and constructive force in his life.

The memory of fears which disturbed them in their youth has often led parents to protect their children from hardships which were a handicap to them. They have struggled to give their offspring the opportunities of which they were deprived.

"We were poor at our house," said a father who was attempting to explain his point of view. "As a boy I never knew what it meant to have more than barely enough to eat. I was never free from the fear of what tomorrow might bring. But this fear played a big part in deciding the course of my life. Because I was both ashamed and afraid of being ignorant I read the best books which I could borrow from the public library. My father's work was seasonal, so we were often reduced to meals which could not satisfy the needs of a growing boy. I determined to search out a type of employment which gave promise of year-round security for my family. The fears which made my youth so unhappy were the driving force which gave me my home, my position, and such blessings as a college education for my daughters."

Fear is sometimes imagined to be a dark monster which waits in the shadows to pounce on its victims. But that picture is false. It misses the essential place which fear has in life. Fear is in some instances a true friend hidden under a dark cloak. She inspires noble efforts, and urges us to accomplish what is worthwhile. Without her we would miss many of life's greatest opportunities.

The ability to see life as a unit is one of the rewards of the Christian point of view. There are no discordant elements in a universe operating under divine law. All of the fundamental human drives come to be accepted as a part of God's providential care. With such a faith, fear is recognized as an agent which is made available to man to protect and encourage him. Used wisely, it gives warning against impending danger, and inspires us to achieve worthy ends.

All of God's gifts are capable of misuse. Love is a word which describes the noblest attitudes of mankind, but this emotion can be distorted until it destroys that which it loves. Ambition sometimes leads an individual to make strenuous efforts which benefit himself and others, but uncontrolled ambition just as often leads to ruin and misery. It is so with fear. It protects us from unexpected danger. It inspires us to achieve goals which otherwise we might never have realized. It is a vivid demonstration of the fact that a wise and loving God is at work in the world.

Sometimes it is difficult to discover the point at which fear ceases to be a constructive force in human development and begins to undermine confidence. Such moments appear in every life. Often they bring unhappiness, tension, and misery with them.

We have considered in this book several of the common fears which are proving a handicap every day to a large number of people. From the analysis of these fears we have discovered a series of steps by which its victims can secure release.

In every case we have seen the need for an understanding of the situation which causes us to be afraid. Many destructive fears have their origin during childhood years as a result of unfortunate factors in the environment. Some develop from persistent defeat in projects which were eagerly begun, but which ended in disaster. Others develop out of a physical infirmity, or from a tendency to magnify a slight weakness until it seems much more of a handicap than it really is.

Endeavor to bring the fear into the light of understanding. To know its source, and to realize its threat to personal contentment, is to take the first necessary move toward control and eventual personal victory.

Second, we have learned that it is necessary to face the fear. Fear multiplies in strength when the issue is avoided, or when methods of escape are contrived. The possibility of release is indefinitely postponed when the mind is closed.

To face up to fear often helps us to discover that its dangerous and threatening hold upon us has been overrated. England's John Masefield emphasized that fact in his poem called, "The Hell-Hounds." Withiel, the hero of the tale, is pursued by fears which the poet likens to hounds in the

157

hunt. He runs until he is exhausted, attempting to escape from their baying fury. At last he can flee no farther. In desperation he turns about and faces his pursuers. He discovers then that the powerful hounds which have seemed about to devour him have been transformed, as if by magic, into a feeble and frail hag, a lifeless specter, which can easily be overpowered.

Many a victim has found that what he fears is weak when he gathers courage enough to face it. While running away, it appears like a giant, but this giant turns into an empty shadow when confronted by the bright light of day.

We have discovered, also, the need to utilize the best knowledge which medicine offers. The discoveries which have been made during this generation concerning the relation of the mind to the functioning of the body offer a hope of healing for all those who are depressed by fear.

Finally, we have learned of the power which comes to those who accept the assurances of faith. Millions of Christians affirm that, whatever one's background may be, faith offers release from fear. Nor is it merely an escape. Christianity sees life as a whole. It recognizes the creative and sustaining power of God. It asserts that His power is sufficient to turn any personal defeat into spiritual victory. It shatters the menace of sickness and death. It offers hope and assurance to those who tremble before the future and its uncertainties. Christianity fills the void which is created by a sense of personal inadequacy, for it promises strength for every need.

Fear is a disease which infects those who live in every part of the world and in every social class. Sometimes it assumes epidemic proportions when national and international tensions prevail. But the cure for such fears has been found. If the healing power is accepted, fear will be restricted to its proper place as an agent at the disposal of man, to warn him of danger and to encourage him to use wisely the powers which have been entrusted to him.

158

REFERENCES AND ACKNOWLEDGMENTS

References and Acknowledgments

CHAPTER I

1. Isaiah 21:11
2. I Kings 19:14
3. Butler, Joseph "The Anthology of Religion," published in 1736; see Preface

CHAPTER II

1. Menninger, Karl T. "The Human Mind"; New York, Knopf, 1930, p. 21
2. From Theodoridas "Palatine Anthology"

CHAPTER III

1. Proverbs 22:13
2. Porter, John J. "I Was Missing Something," Guideposts Associates, Inc., Pawling, N. Y., 1946
3. Exodus 14:13
4. Taylor, Henry J. "Don't Be Afraid," Guideposts Associates, Inc., Pawling, N. Y., 1947

CHAPTER IV

1. Payne, James E. in "Future: the Magazine for Young Men"; September, 1946
2. Shakespeare, William "Midsummer Night's Dream"; Act V, Scene 1, Line 21
3. Prayer delivered by Rev. Peter Marshall in the United States Senate, March 11, 1947
4. Acts 27:25

CHAPTER V

1. Rostand, Edmond "Cyrano de Bergerac," New York, Carlton House, 1923; p. 123
2. Psalms 55:6

CHAPTER VI

1. From poem by James Norman Hall, "Fear"

CHAPTER VII

1. John 3:1
2. From the works of Bayard Taylor (1825-1878)
3. Stone, Irving "Immortal Wife"; New York, Doubleday, Doran, 1944; p. 105

CHAPTER VIII

1. Shakespeare, William "Henry VIII," Act 1, Scene 2, line 88

CHAPTER IX

1. Psalms 102:7
2. II Timothy 4:16
3. Runbeck, Margaret Lee "The Independent Woman," March, 1947
4. Matthew 28:20
5. John 14:18
6. From poem by James Terry White, "Hold Thou My Hands"

CHAPTER X

1. Genesis 15:1

CHAPTER XI

1. Tyerman, L. "Life and Times of John Wesley" vol. 3, London, Hodder & Stoughton, 1888; p. 328
2. Psalms 1:1
3. James, William "The Will to Believe"; New York, Longmans, 1937; p. 84
4. From poem by Thomas Hardy, "On a Fine Morning"

CHAPTER XII

1. From poem by Robert Browning, "Rabbi Ben Ezra"
2. From poem by Edwin Markham, "The Look Ahead"
3. Grenfell, Wilfred "A Labrador Doctor"; New York, Hodder, 1938; p. 97

CHAPTER XIII

1. John 14:9

CHAPTER XIV

1. From poem by Sarah Williams, "The Old Astronomer"
2. Bretz, Alice "I Begin Again"; New York, McGraw, 1940; p. 74

CHAPTER XV

1. From poem by Emily Bronte, "Last Lines"; see Home Book of Verse, New York, Holt, 1926; p. 3486
2. From collection of hymns by Isaac Watts
3. John 11:25

CHAPTER XVI

1. Crile, George "The Origin and Nature of the Emotions"; New York, Saunders and Co., 1915; p. 61
2. Job 1:7